Survivor

Survivor

The long journey
back from abuse

Peter Andrews
Victim No Longer

inspire

British Library Cataloguing in Publication data

A catalogue record for this book is available
from the British Library

ISBN 1 85852 253 6

First published by Inspire
4 John Wesley Road
Werrington
Peterborough PE4 6ZP

Printed and bound in Great Britain by
Stanley L. Hunt (Printers) Ltd, Rushden, Northants

Dedication

This book is dedicated to all victims of abuse and those who support them. Be strong; together we can survive. Don't be afraid to tell the world what happened to you, you have nothing to be ashamed of. The shame lies with those who betrayed you. Believe in yourselves, be proud of who you are and you will find peace in your hearts. The truth will set you free. God bless you.

Foreword

In one sense this book is easy to read. Peter Andrews tells his story well. You get drawn into it. As each chapter ends you want to know what is going to happen next. So you read on.

In another – and far more important – sense, this could be one of the most difficult books you ever read. For while the story is told well, it is a very painful one and you will wish it were not true. Because this is a story of a boy who was let down, betrayed and sometimes abused by people he should have been able to trust. It is not just about adults who deliberately harm and abuse children, though we are becoming increasingly aware of them and the damage they do. Peter's story is also about people who could intervene and make a difference – those who know or suspect that abuse is going on but who do nothing because they are frightened or do not see it as their responsibility to get involved. (The recently set up *Stop it Now* campaign provides an opportunity for people who believe abuse may be happening or who find themselves tempted to abuse children to get professional help and to put a stop to things before they go any further.)

Peter Andrews' story challenges us all. For it is our responsibility to create a safer society – not only for children, but for everyone, particularly for those in vulnerable situations.

As you read this book you may feel hurt and angry at some of what takes place. You may rejoice that against all odds the human spirit has a resilience that enables Peter to make the journey from victim to survivor. And you will probably be relieved that as well as those who ignored the situation or did further harm there are some people in the story who

elp and support. But this telling of Peter's
eally achieve its purpose if, as you read it,
about your own situation and ways in
which you may be able to make our society safer and
more willing to listen.

The book comes as a particular challenge to
churches and Christian organisations. To some extent
this challenge is beginning to be taken up. The Report
Time for Action (Churches Together in Britain and
Ireland, 2002) acknowledges the harm done to those
who have been abused and makes a number of
recommendations on how to respond to the
experience and needs of survivors of abuse. But we
have only just begun and there is a long way still to
go.

The best possible response to this book is not
shock or pity at what went on, but a commitment to
listen to what survivors like Peter have to tell us and
then to ensure that such things do not happen in the
future.

David Gamble

Co-ordinating Secretary for
Legal and Constitutional Practice,
The Methodist Church in Great Britain

September 2004

Preface

This is a true story. All of the people mentio..
are real, but to protect them and their families, the.
names, occupations and the places where these
events happened have been changed. The events that
led to the writing of this book took place in a school
run by a Christian organisation. The name of the
school has also been changed. By so doing, I am able
to tell my story without hurting anyone else.

To begin my journey from being a victim to
becoming a survivor, I first had to overcome the fear,
shame and guilt instilled in me for 30 years by my
abusers. It was not easy, but with the help and
support of others, I crossed that dreadful line and
disclosed what had happened.

Having done so, I then had to face the many
consequences that followed my decision to rid myself
of the terrible burden I had carried all these years,
not least of which was dealing with the nature of
forgiveness.

I finally resolved that struggle by concluding that
it was not necessary to forget in order to forgive, in
fact, the opposite was true. Forgiveness is not without
responsibility. In my case, it was the duty of care to
tell my story truthfully and with such conviction that
others would feel able to tell theirs, so they too can
make the journey and become survivors, free from
guilt, no longer alone and knowing they are not to
blame for what happened to them.

Acknowledgements

There were some who tried to stop me writing this book, but there were many more who made it possible. The debt I owe them requires more than words alone can express, but, for the record, I want to thank my best friend Anne and our three wonderful children, William, Elizabeth and Thomas, for their love, support and understanding through difficult times.

I also want to thank Peter G, Stephen, Robin, Dr Dolan, Helen, Paul K, Sarah, Paul M, Claire, Colin, Dr Price, David, Star, Peter R, Matt, the survivors at Fire-in-Ice and Barnardo's. When the darkness fell, you lit the path and showed me the way.

I would also like to thank my parents. I know how much this hurt you, but it was not your fault. I am still your golden-haired little boy and I will always love you.

Finally, I would like to thank Inspire for their help in producing this book and for having the courage to publish it.

Contents

Prologue

The heron and the kingfisher

In a dream, a small boy sat by a river. On the opposite bank, a kingfisher perched motionless on a bulrush, its head cocked to one side, its right eye focused intently on a group of dark shapes moving in the sparkling waters below. A few yards further upstream stood a heron. It too was looking into the gurgling, bubbling waters.

The boy watched with excited anticipation, waiting for nature's pantomime to begin. Then, without warning, the kingfisher dived into the water like an arrow fired from a bow. A second later it emerged and darted back to the bulrushes, its blue and orange feathers resplendent in the bright, midday sunlight. In its needle-sharp beak, a silvery fish wriggled and squirmed in a desperate attempt to free itself from its fatal predicament.

Then the heron struck. Swiftly, and with great precision, it plunged its long, powerful beak into the water. In the blink of an eye, it withdrew its head to display a much larger fish than the kingfisher had taken. With a single toss of the neck, the heron threw the fish into the air and swallowed it whole as it came down, head first, into its now wide open beak.

A little further along the river bank, a poacher hid among the reeds, his shotgun ready. Without warning, he fired twice: BANG ... BANG. The boy let out a startled cry. His heart raced; he wanted to run, but he was frozen to the spot with fear.

On the surface of the water, close to the bulrushes, blue and orange feathers floated away in silence, all that was left of the beautiful kingfisher. The heron, still alive, thrashed around hopelessly at the water's edge, its right wing blown off at the top joint.

The poacher emerged from his hiding place and walked slowly and silently towards the boy. When he reached the drowning heron, he waded into the shallow water, picked up the dying, bedraggled bird and thrust it into his grubby, bloodstained shoulder bag. He glanced back at the boy once, then walked calmly away, whistling to himself in triumph.

The boy woke up, confused and frightened. He did not tell anyone about his dream, but the images stayed with him through the day. That night he dreamt again that he was back by the river, but now all was dark, save for the stars and the silvery light of the moon that came and went as long, dark clouds sailed across the night sky. Somewhere, out of the darkness, a light appeared in the distance which grew brighter and larger as it came towards him. After a while, the light reached the opposite bank of the river. It was a lamp, carried by a man dressed in a long, white robe. The man raised the lamp above his head with his left hand. The boy could now see his face. It was a kind face.

On his left shoulder sat a large, dark object. The man moved the lamp higher, illuminating the object. It was the heron. The man then stretched out his right arm and opened his fist. Out flew the kingfisher. As it did, the heron leapt gracefully from his shoulder. The two birds flew across the river, alighted at the boy's feet and began calling; the heron with its harsh *'frarnk, frarnk'*; the kingfisher with its shrill *'chee-kee,chee-kee'*. He stared at them with joy. They were alive. They were complete. The boy looked back towards the man, but he was gone. Only the lamp remained. The boy woke up, still confused, but not quite so frightened.

One by one, the years went by and the boy became a man himself. Great joy and great sorrow visited him on many occasions, not all in equal measure. But life's journey taught him much, and, as with all things on earth, time delivers wisdom, and through wisdom comes healing.

One day, at dawn, the man was woken by a sound he knew well. He had heard that sound many times before in his dreams. He got out of bed and went to the window. The sky was turning pink. As he looked out, a large, grey bird flew slowly overhead, turned and glided gracefully towards the river, calling as it went, *'frarnk, frarnk'*. In the willow tree at the end of the garden sat a tiny bird.

The man opened his bedroom window and leaned out. The bird glanced up at him before darting off in a flash of blue and orange, calling as it went, *'chee-kee, chee-kee'*. Suddenly, the sun broke over the horizon, its golden rays setting fire to the clouds. The sky was filled with the light of a million lamps. 'Ah, yes,' said the man. 'Now I understand.'

1

Summer's end

There was no more to be said – it was decided. Subject to the outcome of an entrance exam, I was to be enrolled at Holing Hey College, an independent school for boys. It was August 1963. I was 11 years old and a shy and thoughtful boy. I did not know what to expect nor how to respond. All my parents had said was that I would receive a 'rounded education' in an environment that espoused beliefs that would serve me well in this life and ensure my immortal soul would not be lost in the next. A church school would therefore be the right place for me.

At the appointed hour I was delivered to the headmaster's office by my mother. While she was taken on a tour of the school by an aged teacher, I was escorted up a set of stairs by the headmaster's assistant to an empty classroom overlooking playing fields. The kindly teacher showed me to a desk and beckoned me to sit. On the desk was an upturned sheet of foolscap paper and a pencil. The teacher assured me repeatedly that he had every confidence I would do well in the exam, but I must not look at the questions on the exam paper until he had left the room.

The door closed. I picked up the paper and turned it over. My name was already written on the top, along with the date. I read through the questions carefully, more curious than nervous. I had already failed the Eleven Plus examination, which was why my parents were so keen to get me into this school, the alternative being the local secondary modern school, which, although only 30 minutes' walk from my house, was considered by my father to be a place of such 'poor standards' that I would attain nothing if I went there.

I answered the questions as best I could. I was not a good reader, having struggled to learn to read until the age of eight. Some of the questions were still unanswered when the door reopened and in came the kindly teacher. He told me to stop writing and follow him. The exam paper remained on the desk. A week later, my mother received a telephone call from the school to say that I had passed the exam and I could enrol for the new term starting in September. She was overjoyed. I was amazed – I had actually passed an exam. Maybe I was not as stupid as my father kept telling me. The truth was probably to be found more in the fees my father would pay rather than in the answers I had scribbled down!

September came and I, along with 60 other boys in the new intake, assembled on a windy playground, some with parents, some without, to await our fate. Like soldiers, in our new blazers and caps, we stood to attention, were marked off in a roll call, then led to our classrooms. Mothers, some with the unmistakable sparkle of tears in their eyes, were escorted back to the school entrance. It had begun. Life as I knew it was changed forever.

The days became weeks, the weeks became months, the months became terms. In time, the terms rolled into years. To be honest, those first three years were the happiest days of my life thus far. I made good friends. I did well at my studies. At first, I learnt to love the Church and took great joy in going to services, both at school and in our local church.

By the third year, real friendships had formed. Such is the nature of school friendships, they inevitably spill over into the families of the friends you make. Strong bonds are formed among those families as you grow closer. In Simon's case, our friendship had been slow in developing at first. One of a group of five boys in my class who travelled with me on the train to school each day, Simon and I became close towards the beginning of the third year. He invited me home for a weekend and it was here that I met the most beautiful girl I had ever seen. Sinead, his elder sister by a couple of years. I was mesmerised by her. Totally and utterly lovestruck.

As the months went by, I became a regular visitor to Simon's family. His father, an orthopaedic surgeon, was a wonderful man, kind, generous, funny and loving. In fact the whole family radiated such great affection that, over time, I felt more like another son to them than a school friend. But there was more. My feelings for Sinead became obvious, especially to her mother who, far from trying to dissuade me, encouraged me when I confided in her that I wanted to ask Sinead out on a date, but I was just too scared.

I need not have been, though, as she agreed when I finally plucked up the courage to ask her. From that moment until the onset, 12 months later, of the unimaginable nightmare that lay ahead of me, my life was governed totally by my heart. The joys and mysteries of teenage love – first love – are so precious and wonderful, it would be folly to try and recapture them here as words alone can only scratch the surface. There simply can be no greater joy on earth or in heaven than to be in love with another human being who reciprocates the very same feelings.

By now, many aspects of my development and character had emerged, some good, some not so good. I had proved to be without any skill whatsoever at football or cricket, but I could launch a javelin further than anyone in my year, and I won every archery competition they put up. I could throw things and I could shoot straight – I just couldn't kick a football or bat a cricket ball! Academically, I was not brilliant, but above average; my end of term reports recorded comments pleasing to my parents and pointed to a reasonable future – provided I 'worked harder still' and 'stayed on the same path'.

The religious side of my 'rounded education' proved to be far more demanding than I had anticipated or even imagined. The constant struggle to keep the faith and be free from sin weighed heavily on my soul. The teachers were only too happy to remind us of the constant perils we faced should we give in to temptation. Placing vulnerable, impressionable young children like me under such awful penalties creates a special kind of fear in one that only those who have experienced the same threats could reasonably be expected to understand.

Life at home had a routine of its own. My father worked in the aviation industry and spent weeks at a time away from home in far-flung places. He loved his job and in his own way he loved us, me and my four sisters, the youngest, Annie, having only just been born. My mother ran the house and we all had our own special jobs to do. Mine was keeping the coke boiler going, a task I failed at more times than not. If my father was away, it was no problem. I simply relit the damned thing and life went on. When he was at home, if the boiler went out, serious problems occurred, always accompanied by the usual stream of verbal put-downs that almost always ended with the same statement: 'You're just useless.'

My father only ever beat me once. I have never forgotten it though, as it seemed then, and still does, so unfair. It was not done in the heat of the moment, brought on by some travesty or other on my part. No, it was cold and calculated and delivered hours after the event. I was eight years old and had walked to a friend's house after school instead of going home as I normally did. His mother gave us tea and we played for a while in their garden. At about 5.30, I said goodbye and walked home, a journey of about two miles. It was early July, warm and wonderful.

When I arrived home, I was greeted by my mother who berated me for being so late, demanded to know where I had been and, before I could answer fully, sent me packing upstairs to have a bath, which was already run. As I mounted the stairs, still not fully aware of the drama I had caused, I heard her say that the whole neighbourhood was out looking for me on the common and in the woods. Instinctively I felt that this was not good.

I'd been in the bath for about ten minutes when I heard my father's voice coming from the kitchen below. He sounded extremely angry. Seconds later, he burst through the bathroom door holding a flat piece of wood about a foot long, two inches wide and half an inch thick. Without speaking, he hauled me out of the bath, placed me across his knee, took a towel from the rail, which he placed over my buttocks, and said: 'I'm sorry, but you must learn.' He beat me repeatedly and, despite the towel being between my wet cheeks and his instrument of torture, it still stung in a way I had never experienced before. When it was over, I was sent to my room and told to stay there until called for school the next morning. I didn't cry for long and the warmth of my bed, my sanctuary, soon eased my troubled and confused mind and I drifted off to sleep. Not so many years later that very same bed was to become a place of danger; my sanctuary no longer.

2

Groomed for the taking

The fourth year began much as the third had ended. We were still in the same classroom for now and would remain here until year five. Previous years had involved moving to a new classroom each year, as if to underline the fact that you really were going up, moving on, developing, progressing. There was one change we had not expected; the arrival of a new teacher – Henry Cuthbert Sealy.

Sealy joined the school staff to teach Physics and Chemistry. He seemed at first to be a nice enough man, average height, dark hair, quietly spoken and a refreshing change from the dowdy old teachers who had taught us thus far. Why he chose me I still don't fully understand. But he did, and the awful consequences that followed are the reason for this book.

I was about 14 and a half years old when it began. I was walking towards the station after school one afternoon to catch the train home with my friends. Along the way we passed one of several houses owned by the school used to accommodate those members of the teaching staff who did not live in the main school buildings, along with the boys who boarded at the school. As we passed the gate, there was Sealy in the small front garden, cleaning a large motorcycle. We stopped and asked him about the bike. He told us all sorts of details such as its top speed, engine capacity, how fast he had ridden it; all of the stuff teenage boys want to know about such things.

Mindful of the time, Simon said we should hurry on or we might miss the train, he having the longest journey of us all. As we bid Sealy goodbye and began to move he looked directly at me and asked if I would like a ride home on the bike. Before I could answer, Michael, another of our group who sat next to me in class, butted in saying he would love to ride on the bike. Sealy dismissed him, saying that as I lived in the direction he was planning to go in anyway, he would prefer to take me. This we all agreed was reasonable, so, enviously, my friends all wished me good luck and went on their way.

Sealy went into the house, emerging a moment later wearing a long tweed coat, leather gloves and goggles. He was carrying a gold coloured crash helmet which he placed on my head, then drew me towards him with the strap which he fastened tightly under my chin. I had never been on a motorcycle before, so the thought of what was about to happen filled me with a mixture of excitement and alarm. What would it be like? How fast would we go? Would I be able to speak above the noise of the engine so that I could tell him which way to go? My mind raced. Sealy started the bike, climbed on and gestured to me to climb on behind him. The engine revved up and we roared off down the road towards the station, passing my classmates as we rounded the bend. I hung on for dear life as we sped past them. In a flash they were gone and we headed out towards the dual carriageway, gaining speed with every second.

By the time we reached my house I was shivering with cold, but the exhilaration was such that I didn't even notice. I climbed off the machine and took off the helmet. Sealy muttered something about wearing a coat next time, but before I could say goodbye, he had turned the bike around and roared off down the road, leaving me still holding the helmet.

During the autumn months that followed, Sealy regularly took me home on the bike, stopping from time to time to have a cup of tea. My mother thought he was a nice young man, well-spoken, unassuming, quite charming in fact. The fact that he was spending so much of his time with me seemed not to worry her. But then why should it? He was my teacher after all.

At school, Sealy insisted I sat at the front of the class where he could 'keep an eye on me'. Well, that's what my housemaster told me Sealy had given him as the reason when he requested I be moved. Sealy had also picked up that I was not too good at cricket, so he offered to give me net practice in the playground, every day. I wasn't aware of it at the time, but my classmates noticed that he was always near me at playtime, either talking to me or knocking a football about with me or bowling to me in the nets, which were always left up right through the autumn term until we broke up for the Christmas holiday.

I became very interested in Chemistry as we learnt more about the subject. Sealy told me I was 'gifted' and he offered me extracurricular lessons after school, subject, of course, to my parents' consent. I told my father about it and he seemed keen for me to take up the offer. He instructed me to ask Sealy if he also taught Maths. He did, so my father suggested to Sealy that he would like to pay him to tutor me for private lessons, one evening per week. Sealy agreed, but stipulated that the lessons should be at my home, and, for the sake of convenience, he would bring me home after school on the bike. After the first few lessons, which were conducted on our dining room table, Sealy suggested to my parents that it would be easier if the lessons could be conducted in my bedroom where it was quieter. The reason he gave was that I seemed easily distracted by other things in the house which made it more difficult for him to teach me. My father agreed. That decision was to haunt him many years later.

Christmas came and went and the new year
unfolded upon us. Once back at school, Sealy was
keen to pick up where we had left off at the end of the
previous term. He began to ask me a lot of questions
about Simon and his family. He told me that I should
spend less time with them and concentrate more on
my studies. He was particularly interested in my
feelings for Sinead. He was adamant that I was too
young to be involved with a girl and, in any case, she
was probably not serious about me at all. He often
talked about a girlfriend he had once had who had
really let him down. He never told me her name, nor
anything of substance about her. I couldn't know it at
the time, but I think he was really talking about his
mother.

As Easter approached, plans were made for a
school trip hiking in Wales. About eight boys from my
class signed up, together with a couple from the form
above us. Although not involved in the trip himself,
Sealy was keen to know all about our plans,
particularly where we would be staying and who
would be in charge.

We travelled by train to Chepstow where we
stayed the night in a youth hostel. Over the following
few days we hiked through the Brecon Beacon
National Park to Brecon before finally making our
way back to Abergavenny for our last night. The
following morning, much to everyone's surprise,
Sealy turned up at the hostel and joined us for
breakfast. He said he had been visiting relatives near
Abergavenny and thought he would come and find us
to see how we had got on.

The teacher in charge of us seemed unconcerned
when Sealy asked if he might take me to see Sugar
Loaf mountain. There would not be time, he was told,
so he simply said that would be OK as he could take
me home by road afterwards on his motorcycle. He

told the teacher that my parents were happy about me riding pillion with him as he had taken me home from school on a number of occasions.

I was delighted when the teacher said I could go. Sealy had promised me before that one day he would show me just what the bike could do. This might be the time, I thought. The ride to Sugar Loaf mountain was brilliant. Sealy even rode the bike up the tracks that wound round the mountain itself until the gradient became too steep to negotiate. We stopped here and he produced sandwiches and a flask of hot soup from his grubby haversack. As we ate, he began to talk about his lack of friends, especially girlfriends. He said that he had had difficult relationships with a couple of girls and he asked me if I still had a girlfriend. I told him that Sinead was at boarding school, but she still wrote to me regularly and told me each time that she loved me. He went very quiet for a time and then said abruptly that we should go as it was a long journey back.

The journey home seemed to take a long time. We stopped twice to get fuel and stretch our legs. I was numb with cold, but still enjoying the ride. He didn't say much; just asked me if I was all right and casually told me that we had topped 100 miles per hour several times over the last 80 or so miles. I was elated and could think of nothing else than telling my classmates when I saw them again. They would be green with envy.

In fact, many years later, one of them told me that far from being envious, they were all very suspicious about the fact that Sealy seemed to spend so much time with me. It would be a very long time indeed before they found out that their suspicions had been well founded.

3

The death of innocence

When school began again after the Easter holiday, Sealy arrived driving a second-hand car which he said had been his mother's. He still lived with his mother at weekends and during the school holidays. After school that day, he offered to give me a lift home in the car, but before we went, he said, he wanted to show me something he had made in his laboratory at home. He took me to the playing fields where he produced a small canister which he pressed into the grass.

'Stand back,' he said, as he bent down and lit a small fuse that protruded from the top of the canister.

'What is it?' I asked.

'A smoke bomb,' he said, with a grin.

I was expecting it to go bang. Instead, it fizzed violently for a second or two and then started to give off clouds of thick, grey smoke that rose rapidly into the air and, within a few minutes, completely obscured from view the school buildings on the other side of the field. Sealy beamed. I became anxious, thinking surely we would get into trouble for this? But Sealy assured me that it would be OK. The device had contained a mixture of naphthalene, sodium chlorate and castor sugar – a lethal explosive if mixed in the wrong quantities.

Fortunately for him, but not for me, his ability as a chemist was considerably greater than his judgement. We were challenged once back at the school by the headmaster who demanded to know what we had been doing. Sealy gave the excuse that he was demonstrating an experiment that I had asked for help in understanding. The head accepted the story but said that in future all such experiments must be conducted in the gas chamber in the school lab. It was the first time I had heard Sealy tell a blatant lie. It would not be the last.

The journey home in the car was uneventful until we were about two miles from my house. Sealy, who had hardly said a word since we left the school, asked me casually if I masturbated. It took a few seconds for the words to sink in. I wasn't just shocked – I was totally stunned. I muttered something inaudible, but he insisted, 'Do you masturbate?' I said yes, hoping and praying that my answer would be an end to the conversation. It wasn't, of course, merely the beginning of my nightmare. A nightmare that at times would seem as if it would never end.

'How do you masturbate?' Sealy inquired. I said nothing and turned my head away and looked out of the nearside window. After a moment's pause he began to talk about sex. I continued to stare out of the window. Suddenly, his left hand was on my right knee. Then it was on my crotch. I told him to stop.

'Don't be so silly,' he said. 'It's just a bit of fun. It won't do you any harm. You'll like it.' Never had the last few hundred yards to my house seemed such a long way. It was more like a hundred miles.

I went straight up the stairs to my room and shut the door. My mother asked if I was feeling OK. I told her that I felt a bit sick, but I'd be alright in a while. She didn't see me again until the following morning when I failed to appear for breakfast.

'You'll miss the bus,' she yelled, from the bottom of the stairs.

'I don't feel well,' I replied. 'I want to stay home today.'

My mother came into my bedroom and told me to get up and get to school. I dragged myself out of bed muttering darkly about intense stomach cramps. She would have none of it. That day I kept out of sight at school as much as possible. Fortunately, we didn't have Chemistry so I was able to avoid seeing Sealy until home time. He approached me as I made my way out of the main gate.

'A word, boy,' he commanded. I stopped and he took me to the side of the path to let the other boys go by. When they had passed he asked if I had said anything when I got home.

'About what?' I asked.

'You know,' he said, 'what we were talking about yesterday, on the way home.' I told him that I hadn't spoken to either of my parents.

'Good,' was his reply. 'It might cause a few problems if you mentioned anything like that. Best to keep such things to ourselves.'

Sealy left me alone for a few days after that, but it was not long before he reminded me that I was due another Maths lesson at home, and he was free the next evening. My father had paid in advance for the lessons so I knew there was little chance of me trying to get out of it. The next day, Sealy took me home in his car and, after talking briefly with my mother about the good progress he thought I was making, we went up to my room to begin the lesson. It wasn't a lesson about Maths. Sealy shut the bedroom door, sat me on the chair and put his hands on my crotch and fondled me. He then took my right hand and placed it on his crotch. I pulled my hand back but he grabbed it and held it against his crotch, and began to rub. The look in his eyes was cold. I was terrified. By the time the 60 minute lesson was over, he had masturbated me and forced me to masturbate him.

His trap was sprung. There was no way back. I had died and gone to hell.

Over the months that followed, Sealy would find as many excuses as he could think of to get me on my own. He became more and more demanding as time went on, each time reminding me of the awful consequences that would result if I ever breathed a word about 'our little secret'. The more I tried to dissuade him, the more he would threaten me. His fear tactics comprised a complex package that ranged from him 'committing suicide', for which I would be blamed; me being sent to prison; or him harming us both in some sort of 'freak accident' involving his car. From time to time he would also throw in the fact that no girl, and certainly 'no girl like Sinead', would ever want to have anything to do with me if they were to find out about this.

The combination of direct threats and indirect consequences was more than sufficient to guarantee my silence. I was his toy, a devil's concubine, completely and utterly under his control. He began to tell me in advance when he would next want me to masturbate him, and which school building he would be taking me to. He relished the ever-increasing risks he was taking.

On one occasion, we very nearly got caught. He had taken me to the house where I'd first seen him with the motorcycle. There was no one else in when we entered so he quickly took me into his dingy little bedroom at the back of the house on the ground floor. He stripped off completely and told me to do likewise. It was cold in the room, but, as always, I was already numb with fear, so I didn't really notice the cold at first. He lay on his bed and stretched out, rubbing his penis for a moment before telling me to climb on top of him and sit on his legs, facing his feet.

As I did so, I could hear him breathing faster and faster. His legs were shaking. He let out a loud moan and I felt something wet on my lower back. He had ejaculated over me. I climbed off the bed and he wiped me down with a handkerchief. I started to get dressed, but he pulled me close to him and cuddled me. I felt sick. His hand was soon at work on me and I just let it happen rather than resist. I knew that once it was over, I could go home. It was always the same. Lots of threats leading up to the event, then meaningless chat afterwards. So sure was he of his grip of fear on me, he stopped reminding me about the consequences of telling anyone.

When it was finished, we got dressed and he opened the bedroom door and looked out.

'OK,' he said. 'It's all clear, let's go.' As he moved into the hallway, the front door opened, and in came my English teacher. He looked at Sealy, and then at me standing beside him.

'What are you doing here?' he asked. Sealy casually said we just came in to get a Maths book.

'I teach him at home – we're on our way there now.' Sealy hurried me out of the house. I was terrified.

My performance in school had dwindled to the point that it was being noticed by other teachers. Comment such as 'mind often seems elsewhere' and 'after such a promising start, Peter's work gives cause for concern' began to appear in my class reports. I had also long since stopped going to church. I became withdrawn and reluctant at home, my father putting it down to me being a 'bloody-minded, idle teenager'. My mother said little to me other than I should buck my ideas up and stop moping about. How were they to know? I certainly couldn't tell them; after all, as Sealy repeatedly told me, 'You'll never be believed even if you do say something'; such was his confidence.

Up to now, the abuse had involved only masturbation, bad enough though that was. I was not even aware that there were other forms of sex, such was my naivety. One day, he asked me if I had any thoughts about oral sex. I wasn't sure what he was talking about, so I said, 'Not really'. He began to talk about it, at first in sparse detail, but then in more detail until I was fully informed. His final comment on the subject was that he was not that keen and would prefer just to masturbate me, and me him.

After what seemed like two eternities, school finally broke up for the summer holidays. It was over, I thought. I was so wrong. A week into the holiday, Sealy phoned and asked to speak to my mother. After a brief chat, she put down the phone and called me.

'Mr Sealy is going camping in Wales and he wanted to know if you would like to go with him.' I looked at her, desperate for her to see the fear in my eyes. It was hopeless. If I didn't go, I would go to prison, Sinead would find out, and when I died, I would go to hell. I packed my rucksack and waited for him to collect me.

Sealy was not a man gifted with a sense of humour. He was forever moaning about how unhappy he was and how people had always let him down in the past. On the journey to Wales he asked me several times if I loved him. I knew that 'No' was not the answer he wanted to hear.

'Yes, of course,' I said.

'Good,' he replied, 'because I really love you.' My black soul turned even darker inside. I thought about jumping out of the car to my death. Better to get it over with now and get to hell before he could hurt me any more. I was going there anyway, so what difference did it make?

Our first stop was to call in on the relatives Sealy had said he had been to see before he had collected me from Abergavenny the previous Easter. They were a nice couple, in their early fifties. The man offered me a cigarette. I didn't smoke, but I took it anyway and he lit it for me with a battered old Zip lighter. I took a few puffs and my head began to spin. Waves of nausea consumed me and I stumbled out into the back garden to the sound of raucous laughter behind me. After being sick several times, I went back in and sat quietly in the kitchen. They had stopped laughing now and looked genuinely concerned. Sealy said we should be going soon as he wanted to get to the cottage before dark.

The 'cottage' was in fact a derelict, two-storey stone building that had belonged to a member of his family who had died. Surrounded by acres of woodland, and miles from anywhere, it had not been lived in for many years. There was no heating, no furniture and no glass in many of the windows. It was a wreck.

'It belongs to me now,' said Sealy.' I intend to do it up.' The side door, with its peeling green paint, led to a small kitchen. A rusty old range filled with burnt newspapers and sticks sat on the far wall. A cracked Belfast sink, stained with years of the still-dripping tap, was balanced precariously on a pile of breeze blocks under a filthy window that looked out across the fields beyond.

The stone floor was cold and damp.

'We'll sleep in here tonight,' he said. 'Find some sticks and make a fire in the range. I'll go and get the seats from the car.' By the time I had got the fire going, and he had brought in the old, grey leather rear seats from the car, daylight was beginning to fade. Sealy went back to the car once more and opened the boot. He took out a long object wrapped in a pink striped blanket and a wooden box about ten inches square.

'What are those?' I asked.

'You'll see, come on,' he said.

'Where are we going?' I asked.

'Hunting,' Sealy replied, 'hunting.'

We walked for about a hundred yards into the field directly in front of the cottage. Sealy put down the box and unwrapped the long object. It was a rifle, a .22 BSA. He handed it to me to hold while he bent down, picked up the box and opened it. Inside were some small bullets and an olive green lamp, the like of which I had never seen before.

'What's that?' I asked.

'An Aldis lamp. The sort they used in the Army. Belonged to my father.' He pressed a switch on the handle and the lamp sent out a brilliant beam of light some four inches in diameter, puncturing the now darkening woods around us like a mini searchlight.

The beam seemed to go on forever as it probed between the trees. He told me to hold the lamp so he could load the gun. I shone it towards the edge of the field and there they were.

'Rabbits, dozens of them. Keep it there,' Sealy barked as he raised the gun to his right shoulder. The gun cracked. The rabbits scattered – all of them. He swore and fired again, this time at the empty hedge.

'You missed,' I said with a half laugh. Sealy snapped back that I could probably do no better.

'I bet you I can.' He thrust the gun towards me and looked around.

'OK, let's see you hit the top left window in the cottage.' Sealy shone the lamp on the window. I took careful aim and gently squeezed the trigger. The gun cracked once more and the window collapsed into shards, falling onto the path below with the unmistakable sound of breaking glass. Sealy said nothing and grabbed the gun from me. He fired all of the remaining bullets at the cottage, some hitting what was left of the windows, some ricocheting off the stonework.

He was angry. He walked off back towards the cottage without saying a word. I followed with the lamp. Once back inside the kitchen, he said he was going for a walk, alone. He was gone for about an hour. I was sitting on an old, upturned packing case by the range fire when he returned. It had been raining and he was wet. The anger seemed to have passed. He moved towards the fire and began taking off his clothes. He stood naked for a while warming himself. Then he told me to undress. I knew what was about to happen, or at least I thought I did.

I removed all of my clothes, except my underpants. Sealy pulled me close to him and hugged me in front of the fire for a few moments. The heat at least gave me comfort.

'I want to do something different,' he said.

'What sort of thing?' I asked. Sealy draped his sleeping bag over the upturned packing case and then placed the striped blanket the gun had been wrapped in over the sleeping bag as if to remind me that he still had the gun.

'Lie across the box,' he said. I bent over the box. Sealy began to masturbate. He pulled down my underpants, pushed my legs apart and pressed his penis into my bottom. It did not go in at first and he became agitated and stood back. He then leaned over me and spat on my bottom. I felt his saliva trickling down between my buttocks and over my anus. He pressed his penis against my anus again and pushed into me. This time he penetrated me. The pain was hard to bear and I clenched my buttocks as he pushed further into me.

'It hurts,' I cried. 'It hurts.'

'Just relax', he said, and he paused for a moment. He began again. Moments later, I felt him ejaculate inside me. I will never forget that sensation. My humiliation was complete. I was now a 'pervert'. The reality, of course, was very different. I had been raped.

4

Salvation and betrayal

The sexual and psychological abuse continued through the summer. At my house, at school, in his car, in his lodgings. Anywhere he could take me. My mental health was in serious decline, although I didn't understand at the time exactly what was happening to me. All I knew was that I felt empty, cold, detached, lonely and very frightened. My school work also showed all the signs that something was very badly wrong, so much so, on one end of term report, Sealy marked me top of the class in both Physics and Chemistry to make my report look as if not everything was quite the disaster it really was. In the comment column next to my false marks he wrote: 'An excellent result. Keep it up. Peter cannot afford to relax for a moment.'

His cruel deception may have caused some to pass off the report as 'reasonable', but it did not pass the parent test, and my father wrote in his usual aggressive style to the headmaster to ask why I was doing so badly in my studies. The reply, equally venomous, dismissed his concerns. The war of words had begun. Many more such letters would follow, no doubt written for the moment rather than as testimony to a great wrong. But their authors would see them again, and the terrible truth which lurked behind them would appear many years later, to the shame of the school and the horror of my family. As one old teacher at the school used to tell me: 'Be sure, your sins will find you out. What goes around, comes around.' Well, it most certainly did, but not quite how he had meant.

In the months that followed, I saw Simon and his family from time to time, but much less frequently than before. My relationship with Sinead dwindled like water poured into the sand. This was hardly surprising – I was like a zombie. No one really wanted to know me and I withdrew deeper and deeper into myself. My parents became my enemy. Life was simply awful. Then, out of nowhere, came the most dreadful tragedy. One Saturday, in the autumn, Simon was critically injured in a school rugby game. Two days later, his parents by his side, he died.

For the next two days, I was in complete shock, unable even to cry. Then Simon's father called me at home on the phone to ask me if I would take part in Simon's funeral service. He said there would be only two readers – me and Simon's older brother, John. He added that the service would be taken by a close family friend of theirs, and Sinead's godfather. I had met him on several occasions at their home and he certainly knew who I was. I told Dr Collins that it would be an honour and I would try not to let him down. He thanked me and said it was what the whole family wanted. I put the receiver back onto its cradle and wept uncontrollably.

My dilemma was this: ever since the abuse began, I believed that there was an invisible wall between myself and God. How could I attend Simon's funeral service and even take part in it, unless I had unburdened myself to someone who could assure me of God's forgiveness? On the one hand it seemed obvious to speak to one of my teachers. But, on the other hand, how could I possibly admit that I had been involved in such terrible acts to one of my teachers who knew me well? Questions would be asked and it would all come out. The world around me would collapse. All hope would be lost and I would be an outcast.

But how could I avoid participating in Simon's funeral service? Simon's family would be heartbroken to see me refuse to take part in such an important event in their family life. It was unthinkable. I was in turmoil. What was I to do?

With the funeral only two days away, I made up my mind that I would go and confide in one of the teachers and face whatever consequences there were to be. It was, after all, 'my fault' that I had committed these terrible sins, so I deserved the punishment that was due. The following day, at break time, I made my way across the playground to the main school building and knocked on the staff room door. The teacher who opened it was my housemaster, Mr Swanson.

'Can I see you a moment please, sir?' I said.

'Yes, boy, come in.' There was no one else in the room so I came straight out with it.

'I need to speak to you in confidence, sir. It is urgent.'

'Can it not wait until later?'

'No, sir. It must be now.'

'Very well, follow me.' He led me down the corridor and opened a large, oak-panelled door into the school chapel. We would be undisturbed there. He sat down in one of the heavy oak pews and beckoned me to do the same. My heart was as heavy as lead and I choked before I was able to speak. This was the most difficult thing I had ever done and I was afraid of the consequences. Was I doing the right thing? But I had no choice. I had to unburden myself or I could not go to Simon's funeral service, let alone take part in it as Simon's parents had asked me to do.

I began. 'I have had impure thoughts and done impure things, sir.'

'What sort of things?' he asked. I murmured ...

'Speak up, boy! What sort of things?'

'Sexual acts, sir.' There was a brief pause and he repeated my words.

'Sexual acts? What kind of acts, boy?' I started to go through the litany of evil, dirty, disgusting, unspeakable things that I had done with Sealy. He interrupted me: 'Who did you do all this with, boy?' This was the moment. The end had arrived. I said Sealy's name out loud and waited.

'Do you mean Mr Sealy, your science teacher?'

'Yes, him.' There was a further pause.

'Have you told me everything about this?'

'No, sir, there is more.' Explaining the acts was more difficult than I had thought as I was not really quite sure which part of it was my 'fault'. There was a longer pause when I had finished. Mr Swanson began to tell me that these were very serious matters indeed. I knew that. He went on, but not in the vein of telling me off for what I had done. He wanted me to think about the wider issues here. I didn't understand what he meant and I said so.

'The point is, boy, I will obviously need to take this further, but I can't unless you give me permission to repeat what you have just told me in confidence. Will you do that?' Before I could answer, he said: 'God will forgive you, but these are very serious allegations. I cannot do anything, unless you allow me to repeat what you have just told me.' I was so relieved to hear those precious words – '*God will forgive you*' – I would have done anything. Now I could take part in Simon's funeral service. I could take part in the service as his parents had asked me to do. It was done. I was saved.

It was not done at all. It had only just begun. Far from being saved, I was about to be betrayed by the person I had confided in. With my head still spinning with the relief at having been assured of God's forgiveness, I repeated the story again. Mr Swanson asked no further questions and then placed his right hand on my head and told me to go now and not to worry about it any more. He said he would need to speak to the headmaster, Mr Smith, and that I would probably have to see him as well. I didn't care. The heaviest weight in all the world had just been lifted from my shoulders. I was free, and I would tell Sealy what I had done as soon as I saw him.

On the way back across the playground, I saw him in the cricket nets. He was bowling to a couple of boys from the second year. He called me over. As I got closer he saw in my face that something was adrift.

'What's up?' he asked.

'I've told them,' I said. 'I had to for the funeral service tomorrow. I'm taking part in it. I had to.' He looked at me for a moment and then smiled.

'They won't believe you. I'll just deny it.' The two boys in the nets, unaware of the gravity of our conversation, called to him: 'Come on, sir, bowl the ball.'

'OK,' said Sealy, and he returned to the nets. I went into the school chapel and prayed quietly.

The following day, Simon was laid to rest. The solemnity of the funeral service was matched by the sincerity of the wonderful tributes paid to Simon by his family and friends. When it came to the readings, John and I walked together up the three steps to the front of the church and bowed our heads. The church was silent, but my soul was singing. As I turned and made my way back to my place, I looked at Sinead sitting in the front row next to her parents and her two older sisters. Her face was so sad. I turned round, and sobbed quietly to myself.

A few days later, I was taken to see the headmaster after school. There were also two other people, one of the other teachers and someone else whom I had not seen before. The teacher spoke first, introducing the other man as a 'specialist' in these sorts of matters who would talk to me about what had happened. All three men looked extremely glum.

The teacher and the head then left the room and the interrogation began. The 'specialist' wanted to know every aspect of my sexual history – when had I started to masturbate? Had I done anything like this with anyone else? Did I have sexual fantasies? Had I had sexual contact of any kind with any member of my family? The questions came thick and fast. I became very confused and started crying. The 'specialist' paused for a while and told me not to get upset. He then left the room for a moment. When he returned, his tone was friendlier and he talked about how the school would deal with things from now on. I was given strict instructions not to talk to anyone about the matter, including my parents, while they conducted their enquiries. He said they would speak to me again soon and that I was free to go now and that I should go straight home.

The next day, Sealy did not turn up for our Chemistry lesson. One of the teachers who taught the sixth form came in his place, telling us that Sealy was 'unavailable this morning', but would be in school later. After lunch, I saw him in the playground. He was sharing a joke with some of the older boys. When they had gone, I went over to him and asked him what had happened. He looked at me for a moment with his cold, dark eyes, then smiled in triumph.

'I denied it,' he said. 'They don't believe you. I told you, no one would believe you.'

I was unable to speak and walked slowly away. That was the very last time Sealy spoke to me, even in the classroom.

Christmas came and went and the weeks rolled on towards summer. It was year five – GCE exam year. Although the sexual abuse had stopped, the psychological damage was only just beginning to make its impact felt. By now I had withdrawn so completely that my mother became seriously concerned about me. The school had still not mentioned a word of what I had said to my parents, nor had they said anything more about it to me. I began to suffer bouts of intense stomach cramp which our family doctor put down to 'growing pains'. My loss of appetite and subsequent weight loss was put down to pre-exam nerves, 'not uncommon in boys of my age', my mother was told. The doctor prescribed some vitamin pills; my father told me simply to 'buck my bloody ideas up, or there'd be trouble'.

Unbeknown to me at the time, my father had written to the headmaster twelve months previously, in January 1967, to demand to know why my end of term report was so poor. Without exception, each of my teachers had put negative comments about my performance. 'Very disturbing result', 'This result is the product of a lazy approach', 'Not enough interest in class nor effort at home', 'Very capable in the subject, but mind seems elsewhere', 'Careless, capable of much better', 'Still produces results below his capabilities'.

His letter began: 'I am deeply disturbed by my son's appalling end of term report. Its implications for his future are very serious.' The alarm bells should have been ringing very clearly, yet, on 11 January 1967, the head wrote back to my father: 'You say you are deeply disturbed and cannot any longer let this situation go unchallenged. The tone of your letter – even on the smaller points – suggests very strong disapproval. I think I can say that the school has done a great deal for your son in the past four years. If you so strongly dislike what is being done now, perhaps you would prefer to find another school for him.'

Over the following months, my father wrote several more letters, each time receiving a similar reply. It is not hard to imagine then, after I told them what had been going on in the autumn of 1967, the predicament that they now found themselves in. If they were to tell my parents what I had told them, the war of words between them would quickly erupt into something far more serious. The implications for this private, fee-paying school could not be under-estimated. Their decision, to do and say nothing, was unforgivable but, having made that decision, they were stuck with it. When my father wrote to them again on 7 March 1968, some four months after my conversation with Mr Swanson, he said: 'I have studied Peter's term report with the usual mixed feelings. Not one member of your staff has anything encouraging to say regarding his efforts or diligence, and I continue with the impression that he and form 5a spend too much time playing around instead of concentrating on their studies.'

The head replied by return post in his own hand. He said simply: 'Many thanks for your letter of today. Peter has not done too badly in his mock examinations – apart from Mathematics – and he certainly merits the opportunity of sitting for the subjects you suggest. He has a reasonable chance of success in all of them.' This was the very same teacher who had only months before listened to one of his staff breach my confidence and tell my secrets; arranged for the 'specialist' to interrogate me; listened to the debrief after that interrogation and read the subsequent report. Betrayal is the only word to describe the actions of this cowardly man. But he was not done yet. There was worse to come.

5

Years in the wilderness

Without Simon, school seemed even lonelier than before. I saw Sinead a few times after his death, but she had grown tired of my coldness. I had become fearful of all contact with other human beings. Even a kiss was hard to give. I was living in an almost catatonic state; no wonder, then, that at the end of the Easter break, Sinead told me that she had met someone else and that she didn't want to see me any more. Even though I had known for months that our relationship was fractured beyond repair, I was still brokenhearted and totally destroyed. The hatred I felt for Sealy, the teachers, the school as a whole had reached a level that was no longer measurable.

It was in this awful state that I sat down in the school hall on 28 July 1968 and began three days of exams along with the rest of the fifth year. When they were over, we said our farewells and school was finished for the summer holiday. It would be another 36 years before I would see some of them again.

I can still recall vividly the morning my exam results arrived. I was still in bed when my father came into my room and knelt down by the side of my bed. He had a look of sorrow on his face and he spoke in a soft and gentle manner, most unlike the way he normally spoke to me. When he was done, he got up and left the room. What he had told me took a while to sink in, but when it had I felt no emotion whatsoever. I had failed every single exam but one, Art, and even in that I had only just scraped a pass. Eight years of going to school had come to nothing, and who was to blame? Well, me, of course. I was obviously as stupid and lazy as everyone had said I was. There was no future for me now. It was over. I pulled the covers up over my head and closed my eyes tightly. In my mind, all I could see was Sealy's face smirking and sneering at me.

A few days later, my father told me to telephone the headmaster and ask if I could come back to school in September and repeat the fifth year and retake my exams. When I eventually got through to Mr Smith, his voice was cold and empty. 'I'm afraid there is no room for you. We already have 36 in the class. I can't make an exception. I'm sorry, but the answer is no.' This was the second time he had betrayed me, but it would not be the last. There would be a third time, but it would be another 30 years before the cockerel would crow again.

For reasons that I still don't understand, my father would not speak to Mr Smith. Instead, he wrote to the Director of Education at our County Council, determined to 'get something done'. If only he had sat down with me and asked me what was really wrong. I'm sure I would have told him; I was so exhausted with it all – the pretence, the lies, the guilt, the pain. But he didn't and so it went on. His letter was polite and to the point, but it included an important clue, if only they had read the letter more carefully.

'Sir, may I bring to your attention a situation that has just developed regarding my son Peter, 16, who has been a student at Holing Hey College. Consequent upon encouraging 'mock' GCE examinations, and at the discretion and judgement of his headmaster, he was entered for seven GCE O level examinations in June of this year. For reasons as yet unclear, Peter failed six of them – with the lowest possible grades, and I have recently been advised that the school cannot offer him the opportunity to continue his education and resit his examinations.

Peter has effectively been deprived of any hopes of a full education, and is now prevented from continuing his plans for university. This is an unbelievable situation to which I am totally unable to acquiesce. May I respectfully ask you, therefore, to give this matter your personal and urgent attention in order that Peter may continue with his full-time education to A level standard.'

A week later, the Director of Education replied saying that he had written to the headmaster of another local school to enquire if they could consider me for admission, and that if the headmaster of that school was able to admit me, my father would hear from the school directly. In due course, the headmaster of the other school replied. He was very sorry, but there was 'no room at the inn'.

My father, by now exasperated, and still blaming me for my poor effort, told me that I must enrol at the local technical college and retake some O levels. By now I had become so isolated from reality that the next 12 months might as well never have happened. I was living from hour to hour, day to day, not involved and not aware of what was going on around me. At the end of the course, I sat just two O level exams, Biology and English, and I failed again.

My father, unable to comprehend my apparent stupidity, said I could forget further education. I must find a job and look for somewhere else to live. He did not want me living at home any more. Then he said something disturbing and sinister which really got to me, and still does to this day. He said it was not natural for a boy of my age to spend so much time at home with my mother alone in the house. I'm still not really sure what he meant, but if he meant what I think he did, then I was not the only one with a problem.

So began the years in the wilderness, during which I worked as a window cleaner's assistant, a hospital porter, a van driver's assistant, a shop assistant, a cinema cleaner, a gardener's assistant, and numerous other manual jobs. Being tall, strong, well-mannered and intelligent – despite what my school record of achievement said – it was not difficult to get work of this kind, but I found it very difficult to stay long in any job. I was also easy prey for abusers. If I had thought that I was free from the clutches of evil people, I was very, very wrong. But such is the nature of abuse. The more often you are damaged, the more vulnerable you become, and my first job quickly exposed just how vulnerable I was to further abuse.

Jim was a local car mechanic. Everyone knew him. He was also an experienced abuser who had served time in prison for a range of petty crimes. I did not know that then. He was a strong man, despite being only five foot six inches tall. He had boxed as a younger man and bore the familiar facial scars and broken nose of the sport. My mother had told him about my current position and he offered to give me a job with him for five pounds per week. At the time, I was actually very grateful. At least it would get my father off my back.

Things went well for the first two weeks, then one afternoon, we finished work early and he said he would take me for a drink. I was just 17 years old. After several drinks, I felt slightly the worse for wear. I had not eaten anything all day and the alcohol went to my head quickly. He took me outside to the car park at the back of the pub. It was dark by now. I vomited several times and my head spun like a top. He put me into the back of his dirty old Ford Prefect, climbed in after me and raped me before, eventually, taking me home.

Before we reached the house, he stopped the car and told me that if I said anything to anyone, he would hurt me. He might even have to kill me. For the first time in my life I knew the meaning of terrifying fear; it was different from the fear I had felt when Sealy had abused me.

For the next three months, Jim used and abused me in every way he could. I thought up all sorts of plans in my mind to kill him each time he abused me, none of which I was capable of carrying out. I was just too scared. The intimidation continued, then, one evening, on the way home from work, he stopped the car on the same common on which the neighbourhood had searched for me ten years before on that day I had failed to come home from primary school on time.

It was dark. He began to fondle me, then he grabbed my face and pulled it towards him. He kissed me hard on the lips and then forced his tongue into my mouth. His foul breath made me want to vomit. I pulled my head back but he held on and tried to kiss me again. I jerked my head left then right, then left to try and avoid his continued attempts. He became very angry and began shouting at me. It was the now familiar tirade: 'After everything I've done for you, given you a job, looked after you, driven you around, taken you to pubs. I treat you like my own son and this is how you repay me.' Then he said something that made me realise just how much danger I was really in.

'I've got other boys, you know. They'll do anything for me. I pay them. I think they should teach you a lesson.' The next day I told my mother that I was going to look for another job and if Jim called for me to tell him that I was not at home. She didn't seem particularly bothered, but with four other children in the family to look after, including a two year old, my youngest sister, she had more than enough to cope with without having to worry about me.

I cycled over to the next village and went to see Jonathan, a friend whose father ran a DIY shop. I asked him if they had any jobs and, to my delight, his dad said that he could do with some help on a part-time basis, say three afternoons a week and Saturdays. I said that would be brilliant and he said the pay would be five pounds – the same money Jim was paying me, but for fewer hours. I couldn't believe it; I was free from another nightmare, or so I thought.

The new job went without a problem for about three weeks. I really enjoyed it, as Jonathan's parents, both of whom worked in the shop, were always joking and having a laugh with the customers. It was the opposite of the brutal environment I had experienced working for Jim.

Then, one Saturday, Jim walked into the shop.

'I want to see you,' he demanded. 'Outside.' I told him that I couldn't come out now. 'OK, I'll wait till you finish,' he said and walked out. Jonathan's dad looked concerned and asked me if there was a problem. I said no. 'He was my previous boss and I hadn't given him a week's notice before I left. He's just a bit cross with me.'

Jonathan's dad went out of the shop and looked up the road. Jim was sitting in his car a few yards away. An hour later he was still there.

'I don't like this,' Jonathan's dad said. He went to the phone and called someone. I couldn't hear what was being said, but ten minutes later a burly man in a long trench coat came into the shop and took me into the back room. Jonathan and his dad came with them. The man in the coat introduced himself as a detective superintendent. He was also a personal friend of Jonathan's dad. He started to ask me about

Jim and what did I think he was up to. At this stage I did not feel that I was in any jeopardy, after all, I hadn't done anything wrong in my new job. Then came the heat.

'You two are planning to rob this place, aren't you? You're here to case the place and he's going to come back and break in. That's it, isn't it, lad?' I protested with incredulity. But the more I protested the more the detective scoffed at me and repeated the question.

After about ten more minutes of questions, I said, 'OK, I'll tell you what's really been going on,' and I did. When I'd finished, he said simply, 'Right, you and I are going to the police station.' I was bundled outside and stuffed into the back of a police car. Jim was nowhere to be seen. The next four or five hours are still etched on my mind with such clarity that I can still recall virtually every moment of it.

Once inside the police station, I was taken up a flight of stairs and directed to one of three chairs next to a desk on the first-floor landing. I sat down and watched as people hurried past me, some going up the stairs, some going down. After about ten minutes, two men in civilian clothes came up to me and sat down, one on a chair next to me and one on the edge of the desk. The younger of the two was about 25, the other about 40. The younger man introduced himself as a detective constable and gave his name. He then introduced his colleague, saying that he too was a detective constable.

Over the 30 minutes, they questioned me in minute detail about what had gone on, or rather what they said I had 'claimed' had gone on, between Jim and myself. They made few notes, but many crude comments to each other, all of a sexual nature. I was then escorted up to the next floor and shown into a large room and told to sit on one side of a number of desks that had been placed together to form a table about 20 feet square. Two other men came into the room and my original escorts left.

The interrogation that followed was painful and cruel. They appeared not to have believed a word I said. They mocked me and laughed at me when I tried to describe some of the detail of what had happened. After a while, I became upset and began to cry. After several minutes, one of the detectives said: 'Look, I'm not trying to upset you. I just need to be sure.' I looked at him and asked, 'What do you need to be sure about?'

'All this stuff,' he said. 'All this stuff about what you say he did to you.'

'Why don't you ask him?' I said.

'I think we will,' he said, and left the room. A while later, he returned and said I was free to go but I should report back to the police station at 9 a.m. the following morning. I made my way home in a dazed, bewildered and frightened state, dragging my feet with each step. With a heavy heart, I told my mother what had happened. When my father came home, she took him into the front room and spoke to him. I listened in the front hall. I heard him ask her: 'Is he that way inclined?' She said she didn't know. I was devastated.

My father said nothing at all to me that evening. In the morning, he drove me in silence to the police station. I was shown to a small interview room and he was escorted off to see the Chief Superintendent. After what seemed like eternity, he returned and told me that I was to be examined by the police surgeon. A short, stocky man with silver hair came into the room shortly afterwards holding a small, leather Gladstone bag. He pointed to a green cloth screen in the corner of the room and told me to take off my trousers and underpants. I went behind the screen, took them off and waited. He spoke to my father in such a quiet tone, almost a whisper, I couldn't hear what they were saying. He stepped behind the screen and told me to bend over. He pushed a wooden spatula into my anus, removed it and put it in a plastic bag. He then put some lubricant cream on his right forefinger and proceeded to examine me internally for about 30 seconds. It didn't really hurt, but it was uncomfortable.

Afterwards, he told me to get dressed and wait in the room. He left the room with my father and I sat and waited. Twenty minutes later, my father, accompanied by the Chief Superintendent, came back in. To my astonishment, the Chief Superintendent handed me a piece of paper and said I should sign it, and then I could go. I read the document carefully. It was a retraction of the allegations I had made and an apology for wasting police time. I looked at my father. He too told me to sign it, saying it was in my 'best interest'. I signed it and gave it back to the Chief Superintendent. Apparently, the medical examination had shown no signs of injury, and Jim had, of course, flatly denied the offences when the police had gone round to see him the previous evening. They told my father that they would, however, 'keep an eye on him'.

On the way home my father tried to justify the 'deal' he'd done with the police. I should be very grateful for their understanding and helpful response to this very 'difficult and messy situation'. I thought about his 'deal' for years to come. It may have been a good 'deal' for him, and I can understand why he thought it was the best thing for me. But it was not. For me, it was a tragedy. How could I ever tell anyone about what Sealy had done to me? No one would believe me now, not after 'wasting police time'. I would just have to get on with my life and try to forget what had happened. If only it could have been that simple.

I began to see another of my school friends, Philip, on a regular basis. He lived about eight miles away. His parents were absolutely wonderful and they too began to treat me like another son. His sister was also a joy to be with, funny, happy and gorgeous. I shared some of the best times of my teenage years with them. It was a safe house, a kind house, a musical house. A sanctuary from all my troubles. I loved them dearly and still do.

Not long after the police incident, I got a job as a sales assistant in a large store in London, and took a room in a hostel in Notting Hill. I shared the room with two other lads. They were nice enough, but I was desperately lonely. The food was good, though, and I settled into a routine of sorts: going to work, going back to the hostel, having a meal in the canteen and going to bed. Weekends were the loneliest as my two room-mates both went home for the weekends. I stayed there, not wanting to go home.

As I soon discovered, though, a London store was the wrong place for a vulnerable victim of sexual abuse. I was an easy target for the older, more predatory abusers who worked there. One of them worked the lift. Each time I got in it to go to the floor where I worked, he would make sexual remarks to me, even if there were other people in the lift.

As the weeks went by, his remarks became more personal. On one particular morning, I got into the lift, the only passenger. He closed the gates and off we went. Instead of stopping at my floor, the third, he took the lift to the top floor where the staff canteen was. He took hold of my arm and put his hand on my bottom and began to rub it. I pulled away and told him to stop, which he did. My heart was beating fast;

I was desperate to get out. He took the lift back to the second floor and opened the gates. I flew out of the lift, and out of the store. I never returned. 'What is it about me?' I kept asking myself.

The next day, I took a bus to a London hospital and asked if they had any vacancies for porters. I was in luck and after a short interview with the Beadle, I was told to report to the porters' lodge the following Monday. It was the best job in the world. The doctors never spoke much, usually too engrossed in their work, but that was more than made up for by the nurses, hundreds and hundreds of them. I made some good friends. Sinead was also training to be a nurse there. It was the reason I went for the job, but, although we saw each other almost every day at work, our relationship was never the same as it had been in that first flush of young love. The last time I saw her was two years later at her wedding. She looked so happy. I was genuinely pleased for her, despite my broken heart. Not long afterwards, her elder sister, who had also been a nurse at the hospital, was drowned in a boating accident in Canada. When her mother phoned me to tell me the dreadful news I was unable to take it in. She asked me if I would come to the funeral. I said yes, but I did not go, I just couldn't bear the pain. I have not seen them since and I still feel terrible that I didn't go to the funeral. I know that when they read this book, they will understand.

On my nineteenth birthday I was invited to a party by a staff nurse from the X-ray department, where I'd been working for the previous three months. Susan was short, gently spoken and very pretty. I had spoken to her often in the department, but there was never anything in it apart from work, well, that's what I had thought anyway. I did not know many other people at her party, but I stayed until the end. We had not said much to each other during the evening, but towards the end, when most people had gone, I was sitting in the garden next to the remains of the barbecue fire. She came up to me and asked if I had enjoyed the party. I said yes, it had been fun, and I thanked her for inviting me. She sat down next to me and, without saying anything else, leaned her head on my shoulder. I stayed motionless for a few moments. I did not really know how to respond. The truth was that I was frightened witless.

The abuse I had suffered had made me desperately scared of physical contact. Not surprisingly, I had not been physically close to a woman since my relationship with Sinead before the abuse began. In fact, I found it very difficult to even kiss a girl. I felt awkward and clumsy. For a while we sat there, saying nothing. Then, as if guided by a force I could not see, I took hold of her hand and held it tight. She did not recoil, she did not speak, she just leaned towards me and kissed me gently on the cheek. Over the next few weeks, I spent more and more time with her. I would see her at lunch in the staff canteen almost every day. She would either come and sit with me, or ask me to join her and whoever she was with. I grew very fond of her and found myself thinking of little else. I began to tell her more about myself, not about the abuse, but about my earlier life. She asked me about previous girlfriends. I told her about Sinead. Susan knew who she was, but didn't know her to speak to.

Towards the end of November, she asked me what I was doing over Christmas. I said I had no plans, but I wouldn't be going home. She asked me if I would like to spend it with her at her flat as she would be working on Christmas Day so she wasn't going home either. It was the beginning of what would become the first period of normality in my life since I was 14. Susan helped me through my difficulty with physical contact. She was patient and loving, and when we eventually made love for the first time, she did everything she could to help me overcome my fear, shyness and inexperience.

A month or so later, Susan asked me if I would like to move in with her. There were four other nurses in the flat and they all had boyfriends who spent a good deal of time there, especially at weekends. I jumped at the chance. It was the best thing that could have happened to me and I spent the next 18 months without a worry in the world. We went camping together in Greece in the summer. It was quite magical and, although her parents did not like the idea of us living together, they never mentioned it whenever we went to see them.

Sadly, for me anyway, Susan was offered a chance to work in a hospital in Innsbruck, something she had always wanted to do as she loved to ski. I couldn't ski to save my life, nor could I speak German, whereas Susan was almost fluent. We agreed it was too good an opportunity for her to miss, and, after all, it would only be 'for six months'. I went out to see her the following Christmas. It was a disaster. I moped about like a lost child while she did her best to make me feel wanted. Things had changed and we both knew it. A while later, she wrote to me saying she had met someone else and that she wanted to stay on for another six months. In my heart I knew it was all over. I cried for days.

Rejection is not easy for anyone, but for victims of abuse it can be especially difficult as the impact can be magnified out of proportion, often leading to self-destructive behaviour. In my case, as is not uncommon with victims of sexual abuse, I became extremely promiscuous and began to drink excessively. Over the next three years I changed jobs frequently and had one affair after another, often with women much older than I was. I felt safe with older women and less vulnerable to rejection. Looking back, I can see now that I was just desperate for affection, sex being a way to pretend that I was loved. In reality, I had become sterile in emotional terms, incapable of sharing any real feelings. I had hidden my ability to care deep in my mind to avoid being hurt.

I got a job driving a truck for an international haulage firm. It took me all over Europe and to parts of the Middle East. I met many people, some kind, some not so kind, but I managed to steer clear of people who wanted to harm me. It was a fascinating time, but driving a vehicle over long distances, alone, can be very soul destroying and I was often desperately lonely. After finding myself stuck in Calais, waiting for the ferries to run again, on two successive birthdays, I decided I just wanted to go home and stay there. But where was home?

Back in London, I met a girl called Penny. She had also been a nurse at the hospital. I knew her vaguely from my time there and we began to go out together. She was kind, funny and gregarious. She introduced me to many of her friends and we got on well to begin with. After a couple of months, our relationship became intimate. It was more difficult than I had thought it would be. I had grown fond of her. It was not like it had been with the other women I had slept with over the previous couple of years after Susan had left. I was falling in love, and that was dangerous.

Despite the conflict within me, I continued to see her, all the time pretending that things would be all right. She knew nothing of the past, so why should she need to be told? I could start afresh, a clean slate, a new beginning. I was wrong. It wasn't long before I was sleeping with other women as well. It was only a matter of time before she found out, but I didn't care. It was as if part of me didn't want to be happy.

Happiness was something beyond my understanding. I still hurt so much inside, I was incapable of holding on to anything emotional.

Penny had a sister, five years her senior. She ran a nursing home outside of London and Penny went to work for her. I stayed in London, but visited her most weekends. I got on well with her sister, and after a couple of months, she offered me a job as a gardener's assistant. The job was not well paid, but it came with free accommodation at the home. It was June, summer was in the air. I took the job and moved out of London. The home had large grounds with acres of grass and formal gardens. I spent the next two months mowing the lawns by day and drinking and dancing by night with my new-found friends. It was bliss, but a dark storm was brewing in this country idyll.

My feelings for Penny began to wane as I grew fonder of her sister. It could never have had a happy ending, but I continued regardless. As my relationship with Penny's sister developed, it became obvious to others and the whispering began. Before long, the truth was out and all hell broke loose. The end came swiftly and dramatically, and I was on the run again, unable to cope with the disaster I had created.

My parents were living in Bristol now so I called my mother, told her what had happened at the nursing home and asked if I could come and stay with them for a while until I could find a job and some digs. To my surprise she agreed, so I went home for the first time in many a year, taking with me my faithful dog, Tikka, my leaving present from Susan.

I stayed for a few months, during which time I got a job in a factory and a flat at the top of a large, grey Victorian house, not far from the zoo. Despite the trouble I had caused, Penny kept in touch and we saw each other a few times. She was a strong woman, and she had always competed fiercely with her sister. In time, she said she wanted to try again. I could not find it in my heart to hurt her a second time, so I agreed and she moved in with me. I should have been stronger, but I wasn't. Before long I asked her to marry me. I was 23, she was 24. Eighteen months later, we were divorced. The marriage was a nightmare for us both. Constant rows, sexual problems, excessive drinking, violent outbursts and much more. The end came when Penny told me that she had developed feelings for someone else. It was not another man, but a nursing colleague, a woman five years older than she. It was news I simply couldn't handle. It totally destroyed me.

During the final few months of this miserable episode, I had met a woman called Anne. She was also married at the time, but her husband was a violent man who had an even worse drink problem than I had. We became inseparable and decided we would run away, leaving our troubles behind. We rented a house and moved in together. It was a blissful time and nine months later, Anne became pregnant. Six months later, as soon as our divorces came through, we got married.

In the years that were to follow, there would be great joy and great sorrow, but not all in equal measure. Twenty-five years later, we are still married. We have three wonderful grown-up children and one grandson. Anne has always supported me, in spite of all the pain and heartache I have caused her. Her tenacity, common sense, steadfastness in the face of adversity, and her strong Christian faith, have been the cement that has held it all together. It would be many years before I could tell her what had happened to me, but when I did, she was wonderful. She is a brave and kind woman. I owe her everything and I love her dearly.

6

Crisis – the wounds reopen

Despite the 'rounded education' I was promised having come to such a premature and disastrous end, I did have a natural talent. I could write creatively, but I had never thought that I could turn my talent into something more serious. Having been treated as a failure for most of my life, my self-esteem was not high. Success was what happened to other people, not to me. But all that changed suddenly in 1975, when a friend suggested I should contact the editor of a history magazine he worked for and offer to write for them.

To my amazement, the editor commissioned me to write about a military aircraft, which I did. The article was duly published and I was sent a cheque for £75. I was so elated that I started researching about other military planes, and over the next two years, I had written about almost every fighter aircraft there was. I had found something I enjoyed doing and people wanted to pay me for doing it!

Having discovered my forte, there was no going back and, by 1977, I was earning a living writing things for other people who either couldn't write for themselves, or didn't have the time. Brochures, newsletters, company histories, speeches, leaflets, news articles, press releases, reports, plans, manuals – a million words for a million reasons, important, no doubt, to the people who commissioned them, but not really that important in the wider scheme of things.

But the words in this book are different. They are written for the most important reason I can think of – to help other victims of sexual abuse understand that they are not alone, they are not freaks, they are not to blame for what happened, and their suffering was, and still is, very real. Most important of all, it is to show them that they too can make the journey from being a victim to becoming a survivor. It is a difficult journey, and there are those for whom the pain proves too much. It is as much in their honour that I have written this as it is to help those who are still suffering.

For all victims of abuse, the need to survive is the driving force that shapes your life. Your brain develops coping strategies, often without you realising it. These strategies help you forget the past, but they are also harmful. In my case, I developed a complex range of strategies based on more than one personality. On the outside I was someone else, the life and soul of the party, a joker, only the joke was really on me. On the inside I was a mess, my 'black' heart beat on and the nightmares were never far away. When I was with other people, I wore my mask, but when I was alone, I drank heavily, harmed myself and fought with my demons, all of which led to long periods of depression and self-loathing.

To dwell on this period of my life in any greater detail would not further the purpose of this book. Those of you who have been abused all know what I'm talking about, and those who have not will find it hard to understand. 'Pull yourself together' is a lot easier to say than it is to do. It's not that you can't, it's just that you don't know how to. Therefore, I shall move to October 1996, when the dark, sinister memories I had hidden deep in my mind emerged from the background and began to haunt me again.

I'd been hired to write a newsletter for a high-security psychiatric hospital. It was a new subject for me, but the task itself was similar to work I had done for many other organisations, and I quickly learnt the special language necessary to make sense of the stories I was expected to research and write about. I didn't need to be a psychiatrist to do the task, but I did need to be able to spell it. For a couple of months, the job went well.

The people I worked with were doing a very difficult job in a very difficult and dangerous environment. The pressures were tangible, but not overly difficult to deal with. Bad tempers were the most common problems I had to face. Then, one day, early in February 1997, I received a telephone call and was told to come to the hospital immediately. When I got there, I was briefed about a serious problem facing the hospital. Allegations about sexual abuse within the hospital had been made by a former patient. The case was attracting a large amount of media attention to which the hospital management team had to respond. I was asked if I would join the hospital's press office team to help them deal with the media frenzy they envisaged was about to engulf them. Why I agreed still beats me, even now looking back, but agree I did.

Over the days and weeks that followed, I worked at the hospital every day, helping draft news releases, answer press calls, and write briefing notes for the staff to keep them informed of what was happening. A police investigation began and a judicial inquiry was set up under the chairmanship of a retired judge. It was the most difficult and harrowing job I've ever had, partly because of the nature of the allegations, which reminded me very acutely of my own abuse, and partly because the atmosphere became very hostile as people began to take sides, blame each other, or just simply crack up under the strain. I too began to feel the strain. But for me in particular, there was worse to come, much worse.

It started to go wrong towards the end of the summer of 1997 after a series of difficult exchanges between myself and some of the management team at the hospital. Things were said that I found degrading, threatening and hard to deal with. It all sparked off a period of increasing confusion in my mind. I became irritable, tired and short-tempered. I started drinking heavily again and found it difficult to sleep. As the weeks went by, I lost interest in my work and I found myself thinking back more and more to the events of 30 years ago. Memories of the abuse kept popping into my mind. It got worse and I began thinking of little else. It was as if the experience at the hospital had triggered off a process that was unlocking the nightmares I had hidden deep in my mind in a box I had marked 'DO NOT OPEN – EVER'.

When I did fall asleep, I started to have troubling dreams, often involving replays of the abuse. Physical symptoms began to emerge such as night sweats, headaches and palpitations. I became tearful and would cry without warning. I also became very sensitive to criticism and loud noises. I felt increasingly threatened by imaginary problems. I would cross the road to avoid people, especially men. My short-term memory also deteriorated to the point where I would put a kettle on to boil and then walk away and do something else, completely forgetting the kettle. I was in trouble and I knew it. I just didn't understand what the problem was.

In November, the hospital, now under new management, rang me up one afternoon and told me that my services were no longer required. I reminded them that I had a contract which entitled me to three months' notice. They told me they were not going to give me any notice. I hadn't done anything wrong, I was just seen as connected to the old guard, and they were all being replaced. The feelings of betrayal I'd experienced at school, when I was not allowed back after I failed my exams, flooded back. I wanted someone to pay, but who, and how?

For the next 18 months, I struggled on, but I found it increasingly difficult to motivate myself and work became hard to find. I began to borrow money to service existing debts and pay the mortgage. The spiral of decline was now in full flood and my mood swings became more marked by the day. I would spend hours sitting in my study gazing at my computer screen, unable to type a single word. I had also become impotent. It was as if I was dead.

Then, something happened that, although not obvious to me at the time, set in motion the changes in my mind that were to unlock my prison and set me free. My beautiful William, my first-born, my treasure, my little boy, the child I loved so much and had tried so hard to protect from the evils I had endured, left home to go to university. It was September 1998. The loneliness inside me grew like a cancer. I was bereft, empty and drained of all emotion. It was as if he had taken my very soul with him.

One day, I went into his room at the top of the old farmhouse where we lived and sat on the floor. I could feel his presence and it gave me comfort. I opened one of his drawers and took out a grey sweater he used to wear. I put it on and sat on his bed. All the memories of this dear little boy walked their way in procession through my mind. He was not gone, he was just away. For the next five days, I spent every minute in that room, painting it from top to bottom, making new shelves and picture frames, hoovering, dusting, tidying. I bought new rugs and lampshades, new lights for his bedside table, and when that was done, I made him a new bed. It was my way of showing him that, while I knew he had to go, this was his home, he would always be welcome here.

It was during these quiet few days, alone in that room, that I tried to make sense of what was happening to me. When it was over, I knew what I had to do. I knew who was to blame. I knew the way out. I rang my father and told him that I was thinking of writing an article about my school days, and wondered if he still had any old photos or school reports that I could look at. He said he thought he still had 'a few letters' in the loft somewhere. He would dig them out and send them to me.

Three days later, a package arrived, addressed in his handwriting. To my amazement, inside were all of my school reports, right back to primary school, handwritten first drafts of the letters he had sent to the school over the years, and all of their replies, most of which I had never seen before. They were all collated in chronological order and I began to read through them. When I reached my Christmas term report from year four, there was Sealy's handwriting in the section on my performance for Physics and Chemistry. The words on the document in front of me had been written by his hand. The same hand that had abused me, time after time after time. I looked at the words, and my eyes filled with tears. The floodgates opened and I wept and wept and wept. It was as if he was right there, standing in front of me. As my tears poured onto the page and mingled with the ink, I screamed out loud: 'You're going to pay for this, you bastard. You're bloody well going to pay.'

After a while I stopped crying. I turned on my computer, logged into a search engine and typed in the name of the school. Seconds later I was looking at pictures of my old school, the names of the current teaching staff, a guest book filled with the names and details of old boys, including boys in my cohort. I rattled off an e-mail to a few of them asking if they had any school photos of year 4A. Two hours later, a reply from a boy who had sat only a few feet away from me in class appeared in my mailbox. It had an attachment. It was another hour before I summoned the courage to open the attachment. I knew what it was. I knew what it would contain. I was frightened again. I pressed the download command. The computer responded and, there before me, a black and white photo appeared – all my old classmates, my teachers, my abuser, and me. I felt sick and turned the computer off.

Later that afternoon, I phoned a friend of mine, Allan. He was a solicitor.

'Could I come and see you on a rather difficult personal matter?'

'What's it about?' I began to tell him roughly about the things that had happened, but after ten minutes, he said: 'Why don't you write it all down and then come and see me?'

For the next three days, I wrote and wrote and wrote. On the fourth day I went to see Allan. It took him an hour to read through the document. When he'd reached the end, he put the document down and looked at me. 'I just don't know what to say. It's just so hard to imagine what it must have been like all these years living with this.'

'What should I do?' I asked.

'Sue the bastard,' said Allan. 'And sue the bloody school as well, and the sodding local authority. Sue them all.'

Before I could say anything more, Allan took out a piece of paper and began scribbling furiously and barking questions at me. 'What's the school's full address? Who's the current headmaster? Who's the current Director of Education at the Council?'

'What are you going to do?' I said.

'I'm going to write to them and ask them for the names of their insurance companies – that usually gets a prompt response! In the meantime, you need to get a proper medical assessment – you're obviously suffering from all this and we need to know exactly what the problems are.'

'I'll make an appointment with my GP,' I said. I thanked him for listening. It had been obvious during the meeting that he had found what I had to say uncomfortable, but there was now anger in his eyes. I knew he would help me. We shook hands and he showed me out.

7

To mend a broken soul

Dr Carol is a wonderful human being. There is really no other way to describe her. She illuminates a room when she enters. She is also a brilliant GP. I started to tell her my tale of woe. After 15 minutes she stopped me and said that there was no way we were going to get to the root of the problem that morning.

'There just isn't time and you've seen the queue out there!'

I agreed and said I'd come back tomorrow.

'No,' she said, 'I need to understand more about your history before I can help you so I'll arrange for you to see Sally, our Community Psychiatric Nurse. She will climb inside your head and then tell me what's wrong!'

Two weeks later, I had my first appointment with Sally. I had never met an angel before. It was a powerful experience for me, the first of many more I would have in the journey that lay ahead, not all of which would I look back on with the same feelings. Sally took me to a consulting room and sat me down. She talked a little about her role as a CPN and then asked me to tell her what the problem was.

'Take your time,' she said. 'There is no hurry.' I began to spill out my story all over again. I was doing OK until I got to the part when dear Simon's father had asked me if I would read at Simon's funeral service alongside his brother John. When I'd first written it down in the account I prepared for Allan, it was words on paper. But now I was saying it out loud, it seemed so real, as if I was back there on the day.

I felt my bottom lip beginning to give. I began to cry, it was such a relief. I sobbed and sobbed. I just couldn't stop it. It was as if all the pain of all those years had suddenly broken through the dam and nothing could hold it back.

Sally waited patiently until I'd stopped crying and then handed me a small box of tissues. I pulled one out and dried my eyes.

'Do you want to stop?'

'No, I'm OK. There's not much more to the story anyway.' I told her about the other periods of abuse, and then described all the problems I was having now. When I'd finished, she looked at me for a moment, then began to speak, gently, but with command.

'Peter, I am fairly certain from what you have told me that you are suffering from Post Traumatic Stress Disorder. I think you may also have an underlying depressive illness. We can fix both of these problems, but it is going to take some time.' She picked up her phone and called Dr Carol. They talked for a while, then Sally took me into Dr Carol's room and said goodbye.

'Right,' said Dr Carol. 'I'm going to put you on a course of Fluoxetine, you might know it better as Prozac. It will sort out the underlying depression. It normally takes a couple of weeks to fully kick in, but you should begin to feel a change within a few days. You will need to take it for at least six months, but don't worry, that's not a problem. My main concern right now is your blood pressure. How long has it been this high?'

I didn't know. I couldn't remember the last time I'd had it checked.

'Well, if we don't do something about it soon,' she said, 'you won't need the Prozac because you'll be dead!' She had a way with words!

'I will also write to the Psychology Department at the hospital and we'll get you on a course of trauma counselling. They're very good and they have a guy who specialises in sexual trauma. He'll help you understand exactly what has caused the past to re-emerge, and what needs to be done to put it back in its box. Sally will review you every four weeks to monitor your progress.'

Dr Carol tapped some details into her computer and the printer churned out a prescription.

'Take one Prozac capsule and one Aprovel tablet every morning. The Aprovel will bring your blood pressure down to normal levels in a day or two. Any problems, just call me.' I thanked her and made my way to the nearest chemist.

A few weeks later, I received a letter from the hospital asking me if I would be prepared to attend their Psychology Department for an assessment. I replied the same day, but it was another three months before they wrote to confirm a date for an appointment with a behavioural psychologist called John Karrow, who would assess me.

John was nothing like I had imagined him to be. Short and Scouse with a broad smile, a broken front tooth and constantly flicking his hair with his right hand. I quickly grew to like this man, his no-nonsense way of dealing with the issues was a source of great help to me. He was also a Christian, so he understood from his own first-hand experience the complexity of the problems involved.

John asked me to tell him the whole sad story. As I relived my journey to hell and back for him, he took copious notes. When I'd finished, he didn't say anything for a while, reading and rereading his notes. Eventually, he put down the pad and looked at me for a moment as he gathered his thoughts.

'Your story is sadly not unique, Peter, except for you, of course. It is very much unique for you. No child should have to be exposed to such awful experiences, yet it is far from uncommon. The only benefit from that, if you can call it a benefit, is that we are beginning to understand the impact of childhood sexual abuse, because we are constantly being faced with people like you, adults who were abused as children, who, now, much later in life, are victimised again by the re-emergence of the traumas suffered. We call the problems you are currently going through simply the 'crisis', because that's exactly what it is. We can help you overcome this crisis, but it will take time, and before I can work out a programme to help you specifically, I need to understand in more detail how you felt in the past, and how you feel now.' John reached over and handed me a document.

'Don't read this now, take it home and work on it over the next few days. It's a list of questions. I want you to answer them frankly, and in as much detail as you think appropriate. Post it back to me when you've finished and I'll call you for another appointment.' He shook my hand warmly and led me out to the reception area. I made my way home, confused but happy. I was at last beginning to make some sense of all this pain.

I didn't look at the questionnaire for two days. I just felt so washed out; the thought of having to write down my story yet again seemed like a mountain I just did not want to face. In fact, when I did read the document, and saw the logic of the questions, I found writing down the answers was a cathartic process in itself. Each question had a score attached to it. When I'd finished and looked at my answers in relation to the score sheet, it showed that my answers gave the evidence necessary to substantiate a diagnosis of Post Traumatic Stress Disorder, with the degree of the impact on me being classed as 'Extreme'. At least I now knew for sure what was wrong, and it frightened me. I posted the completed questionnaire back to John that afternoon.

A couple of weeks later, he wrote to me saying that he had shown the document to his colleague, David Lander, who had just helped set up a newly formed counselling group at one of the voluntary childcare organisations for men who had been sexually abused. He recommended that I should make contact with him, which I did, but it would be another three months before I got to see this man. By now it was becoming clear that the NHS, reflecting society in general, was not geared to dealing with adult males who had suffered childhood sexual abuse. The abuse scandals now emerging in churches and schools and elsewhere were still in their infancy. This was a new problem that no one seemed to want to get to grips with. Over the coming months, though, the dam would begin to crack and the suffering of thousands upon thousands of young children, abused and betrayed by those who were responsible for their care and well-being, would start to flow. Well-respected institutions would be rocked to their very foundations, and, little, insignificant me would be right in the middle of it all.

On 12 June 2000, I finally met David. He was tall, good-looking and extremely confident, and he put me instantly at ease. I found going through my story with him less difficult than on previous occasions, but perhaps I was just getting used to telling it. David listened carefully, but after a while he seemed to become distracted. It was obvious that he had something else on his mind. When I'd finished, he said this first session was just so we could get to know each other and that the real work would begin next time. He proposed ten sessions, one a week for about an hour. I thanked him and he showed me out.

The next meeting, on 19 June, was the last time I ever saw him. During the session, I did most of the talking, which ranged from my problems with alcohol to the painful and frightening subject of whether or not I would become an abuser myself because I had been abused. David's mobile phone went off several times during the conversation and he would make excuses and leave the room to answer the phone. Each time he came back in, he looked perplexed and distant. I felt very vulnerable and began to wish I wasn't there. Before the hour was up, while I was still talking, David suddenly said he had to cut it short because he had another appointment, but he would see me again in a week and we could pick up from there. I was confused and annoyed, but relieved it was over.

On 23 June, I received a short letter from his secretary saying the appointment was cancelled as David was unavailable until further notice. 'We will be in touch again at the earliest opportunity with an alternative appointment.' I was shattered. Only a few days ago, I had been talking to this man about some of the blackest and most frightening thoughts that lurked in the darkest regions of my mind. Why? Because he had said he could help. Now he was gone. No goodbye, no explanation, just gone.

A month later, I received a letter from John Karrow. It said that David Lander was no longer with the department and I was to contact the office of the organisation in Liverpool myself to make arrangements to attend the Men's Group. He ended the letter with the words 'Good luck'. A week later, having tried unsuccessfully to make contact with the facilitator of the group, I wrote to John to try and explain how I now felt about the whole situation. I said that the unexplained circumstances surrounding David's abrupt departure had left me feeling confused and disturbed. I said that the feelings of being let down again were strong at the moment, but that I was trying to be as objective as I could about it.

A few days later, I saw Sally again. When I told her what had happened, she was so concerned that she telephoned David Lander's secretary and asked them to find me another psychotherapist to continue the therapy David had begun.

On 14 August, I received a reply, not from John, but from his boss, the Clinical Director. He apologised sincerely on behalf of the Directorate for the 'inevitable emotional consequences for yourself', and said he would arrange for me to be seen as a priority for one-to-one psychological therapy. He did, and finally, on 18 September, I began an intensive course of therapy with John Karrow which really helped me make sense of the past and overcome some, but not all, of the fears it had left me with.

A central part of the therapy involved a treatment called EMDR (Eye Movement Desensitisation and Reprocessing). Developed by an American psychologist, Dr Franchine Shapiro, EMDR was proving to be of considerable help in cases for victims with anxiety-based disorders, and disorders that have their basis in emotional trauma in earlier years.

John had just begun to introduce the treatment and he was as keen as I was to try it on me based on positive reports of its success. Before we began, he warned me that I might find EMDR therapy difficult as it involved exploring deep into my memory and drawing out in very minute detail what had happened. I even had to sign a disclaimer saying that if it made things worse, I wouldn't sue them! Despite this, I trusted John and we got on with it.

The purpose of EMDR is to enable painful memories to be refiled in your memory in such a way they become less likely to pop into your mind when you don't want them to. The treatment requires you to close your eyes and focus on three main aspects of the trauma. Firstly, a visual image, which is usually an image you associate with the most disturbing part of the trauma. Secondly, the negative thought you have about yourself in relation to the trauma, and thirdly, the location of the disturbance in your body. You then open your eyes and follow the therapist's finger as it tracks back and forward across your visual field in rapid, saccadic eye movements.

After each set of movements, you report what you are experiencing. As the process continues, you notice a decrease in the emotional impact of the trauma memory. This decrease can be gradual or, in some cases, dramatic.

You may also notice, as I did, that your perception of your own part in the trauma changes. Abreaction can also occur, which is where disturbing memories that have been forgotten or repressed suddenly come to the surface, often accompanied by the release of more painful memories.

The part of the trauma I focused on was the event in the cottage when Sealy first raped me. The image of the fire in the range was so clear, I could even feel the heat. The negative thought I focused on was the feelings I had at the time of being weak and feeble and unable to help myself. The location of the disturbance in my body was my stomach, the place I suffered those terrible cramps for years afterwards.

For the next few months, John counselled me once a week for an hour. Although painful and challenging, the process did work. I recommend it to other victims as I can now think about what happened to me in a much more rational way without it triggering the kind of symptoms I had previously suffered from.

John had also recommended that I should still go along to the Men's Group as he felt it would help me as I would learn about coping with the impact of abuse directly from others who had gone through similar ordeals. The group had been established by the charity following the North Wales Care Home abuse cases which had highlighted the need for such support. I joined and attended the Group which also met once a week.

'Sad school', as my children named it, was also very helpful to me. The conversations in the group, which will always remain confidential, were not easy, but they allowed each member of the group to say things that we found so difficult to say to anyone else, even to our individual therapists. The facilitator who ran our group is a remarkable man. He is a brave and highly skilled family therapist. I owe him a great deal, as do we all in the group. I learnt a great deal from the other members of the group about the kindness victims of abuse can show, despite their ordeals. They all had terrible tales to tell of their appalling treatment, some of which was far worse than the abuse I had suffered. Their courage was humbling and they have been a great source of healing. I only hope that through my contribution, I was able to help them in some small way as well.

8

Stepping out from the shadows

In the months of waiting for the counselling with John Karrow, I had also begun another vital phase in my struggle to recover: the battle for justice, which was to prove every bit as testing as the therapy. The conclusion I had come to at the end of my week in William's room was that I would have to confront the school once more with what had happened to me, but this time I would stand in front of them as a man, not a child. This time I would make them listen to me and apologise for failing me so badly. I was convinced in my own mind that I would never fully recover from my ordeal until I had resolved the question of how unfairly I had been dealt with by the school and others. The sense of betrayal had so stained my character that I had come to view almost everyone and everything in life with suspicion and doubt. If I was going to move on, I would have to find a way of resolving that.

I still carried in my heart anger and hatred for Sealy, the school and everyone who had ever let me down. That anger had long since ceased to be the fiery rage that we all feel when things go wrong. It was a dark anger that had become tempered by time, like steel. It was cold, intense and deadly. I could use it now to save me, or I could let it go on etching into my soul until one day, perhaps, it would destroy me. As I wrestled with this terrifying conundrum, I weighed up all the possible outcomes. I drew up a list of all the bad outcomes and all the good outcomes. The bad included the way people might think of me when they found out. The good included the possibility that if I told my story, others might also be able to tell theirs.

By the time I had written down all of the possibilities, good and bad, that I could think of, the answer began to emerge. I would make a stand and take the consequences like a man. It was time to stop being frightened. It was now or never. I would find a way to challenge Sealy, if he was still alive, and the school, and force them to acknowledge the damage they had done. But I would also challenge them further. I would ask them to prove to me that what happened to me could not happen to other boys now. After all, weren't Christian organisations trying to show the world that they had changed their ways and would not tolerate anyone in a position of authority who abused children?

A few days after I had gone to see Dr Carol that first time, Allan, the solicitor, had phoned me to say that his letter to my old school had certainly stirred up a hornet's nest, but not quite in the way he had expected. Their reply, via their solicitors, was to inform him that they had 'no record of any incident' involving me, and, further, they had no record of any teacher with the name I had supplied ever working at the school. I searched through my old school reports and the letters my father had sent me, which revealed the correct spelling of Sealy's name. I had transposed two letters of his surname – hardly enough to warrant their 'no record of any teacher' response – but enough to show us that we had a fight on our hands.

I was determined to make the school take me seriously this time. Allan advised me to make a formal complaint to the police. He said that there is no time limit on sexual offences, and, as I was not 16 when Sealy assaulted me at the cottage, I was unable in law to give my 'consent', therefore, what he had done to me was statutory rape, which carries a ten-year prison sentence.

'That will get them thinking,' he said. I put the phone down and wrote a letter to the police.

By now, I was able to write my story without feeling so completely overwhelmed, although it was still difficult to read the words as they appeared on the screen in front of me. I explained what had happened at school and how it had affected me. I said that I wanted to stop being a victim, and to achieve this I intended to seek redress through the civil and criminal justice system for the suffering I had endured over all these years. I attached a copy of the document I had prepared for Allan, and said I would be happy to give them any further information they might want. I addressed the letter to the Chief Superintendent at the police station nearest to my old school, and posted it. It was done. I had lit the fuse. No more mealy-mouthed letters from the school's solicitors. The gloves were well and truly off now, and I felt a sense of calm growing inside me. I was no longer fighting my battle on my own.

Three days later, I received a short letter from the police asking me simply to telephone them. It was signed WPC Susan Miller, Child Protection Unit. It made no mention of the subject so I called her as soon as I had finished reading it. She explained that they needed to be sure it was me they were talking to and not some crank who had used my address. She said she had been tasked with investigating my allegations and suggested we meet at their special interview house which, although designed for interviewing children, was very private and had all the necessary recording facilities. We agreed a date and time and she said she and a colleague would collect me from the train station when I arrived.

The journey down was a roller-coaster of emotions. I was unsure how I would react in the interview, given the last experience I'd had with the police, but I felt happy that at last something positive was happening. I took with me my old school reports, the letters and the school photograph. At this stage I still did not know if Sealy was alive or dead.

Susan was about 30, tall and quietly spoken with a soft West Country accent. Her colleague was a little older, not quite as tall and spoke with a harsher northern accent. They were both so different from the two male detectives who'd interrogated me all those years ago about Jim. The special house, a converted police house in a quiet residential street in suburbia, was filled with toys, children's books and videos. It was perfect and I felt instantly at ease. I had met another angel.

For the next four hours, Susan delved deep into my past, dragging out every last scrap of information about me, my family and Sealy. She was a highly trained and skilful investigator. I was amazed at some of the information she was able to unlock. It was the level of detail in particular that made such an impact on me. Questions like: 'What did you use to clean up after he had abused you?' Until she'd asked me that I hadn't even thought about it.

'His hanky,' I said. 'A white hanky – I can see it now.'

Her colleague said very little during the entire interview; her unenviable task was to write down everything I said. We had to stop several times due to cramp in her fingers. In the end, when Susan was satisfied that she had retrieved every last piece of information from my memory, she asked me if there was anything I wanted to ask her.

'There is something that still bothers me,' I said. 'From all that I've told you, do you feel in any way that I was to blame for what happened? Could I have stopped it from happening sooner?' Susan looked at me for a moment and said: 'Peter, you were a child. He was an adult and your teacher. What else could you have done in reality? Nothing. He is entirely guilty for what he did to you. It was not within your power to stop him. You were not to blame in any way whatsoever, and that's all there is to say about it.'

I began to cry, more out of relief that it was all out in the open, but partly because of the image burning in my mind, the image of me staring back at myself from the school photo. A young boy. A child. She was right. I'd done nothing to be ashamed of, yet I still felt ashamed. I gave her the photo and they took me back to the train station.

'I'll call you in a few days when we've typed up your statement. You'll have to come back to sign it if that's OK. In the meantime, we'll begin making our "enquiries" as they say!' I thanked them both for the way they had conducted the interview and climbed aboard the waiting train. It had been a difficult but positive day.

It would be some time before I learnt that Susan's 'enquiries' had shaken the school to its foundations, and in doing so, she had uncovered disturbing circumstantial evidence that, on the face of it, looked very much as if the school had gone out of its way to cover up what they knew to be true to avoid a major scandal.

With a police investigation underway, the school's solicitors suddenly became much more amenable, assuring Allan, who was now acting officially for me, that they were not in any way trying to be obstructive when they had failed to recognise the correct name of the teacher. Now that the police were involved, however, the civil action would have to wait. No matter; we now had their full attention. Now was the time to tackle those further up the chain of responsibility. I wrote to the Director of Education at the County Council to ask him to set up a formal inquiry into all of the issues involved in my case.

I told him the whole story and added that I had given a statement to the police. I wanted to embarrass the council into explaining why my school had been able to get away with keeping my 'disclosures' hidden. I put it to him that here were fundamental questions that needed answering, such as, did the school properly investigate my allegations at the time in accordance with the regulations and procedures covering such incidents? What action did the school take following their investigation? Why had I not been offered counselling and support? Why were my parents not told? Why were the police not told? Why was I told not to say anything further about it? Why was the teacher who abused me not suspended? What action was taken to ensure that this teacher did not further abuse me or any other pupil and, finally, what lessons can be learnt to ensure that what happened to me cannot happen again to others?

The council's education policy was spelt out very clearly on their web site. They proudly boasted that their 'aim for school education was to ensure that each pupil reached his or her full potential, and to secure the highest possible standards of attainment for all, through a broad and balanced school education which prepares pupils for the responsibilities and opportunities of adult life'.

I suggested to the Director of Education that it was reasonable to assume that this policy, albeit not published on a web site, was also in place in 1966, but what had happened to me severely damaged my chance to reach my full potential, denied me any opportunity of securing the highest possible standards of attainment and failed absolutely to prepare me for the responsibilities and opportunities of adult life.

'The truth is,' I told him, 'I was denied the opportunity to reach my potential, or get anywhere near reaching it, by the very people who were entrusted in law to provide me with the pastoral care, appropriate learning environment and adequate support necessary for me to thrive.' I finished by saying that I had set myself six objectives as part of my recovery process, and that I would not rest until I had achieved them all. I wanted the school to accept that I was abused, to accept that they failed to protect and support me and to accept that they had denied me the opportunity to reach my full potential. I also wanted a sincere apology, some form of compensation and an assurance and evidence that what happened to me could not happen again to others. I knew that my letter would cause them difficulties, but I also knew how devious and treacherous bureaucrats could be so, to make sure my letter did not get 'lost in the system', I sent a copy to the Secretary of State for Education.

A week went by and I had not had any response, so I wrote again to the council, and this time I also wrote to my MP, enclosing a copy of a letter I had sent to the Director of Education, and asking if he would also write to the council on my behalf and ask them what they intended to do about the issues I had raised.

On 27 January, the Director of Education replied, saying that he was very disturbed to read my letter, and that he had 'immediately referred the matter to my colleagues in Social Services whose responsibility it is to conduct investigations of this nature'. Now that I had his attention, it was time to put a spoke in the wheel. I wrote back on 31 January saying that, in preparing my case, I had discovered extensive correspondence between my father and the school, and the Chief Education Officer at the time, covering the period of the abuse and beyond it. I told him that it was very clear from this correspondence that it was obvious at the time that something was seriously wrong with my progress, yet neither the school nor the then Director of Education had given any indication to my father that I had in fact informed the school that I was being abused.

Had he been told, of course, the reason for my lack of progress would have been obvious to all, as indeed would the likely outcomes and consequences that would then have followed. I put it to him that, in my view, the difficulty the discovery of this correspondence posed is that it raises the question of what exactly did the Education Department know at the time about my situation and what action did it take? 'Your department clearly should not be involved in investigating itself, and I am therefore asking you to assure me that the Child Protection and Independent Review Unit does in fact have the authority to investigate independently your department's involvement in my case as well as the authority to investigate the school's involvement. I am not suggesting that the Education Department did in fact know about the abuse at the time, but I'm sure you will appreciate my concerns.'

Having had no reply by 7 February, I telephoned the contact I had been referred to by the Director of Education at their Child Protection Unit. He seemed uncomfortable and not really sure what to say to me.

'Basically,' he said, 'I've been given your case because it's got "child protection" written all over it, which is absolutely appropriate. We now have some procedural guidance which our area child protection committee has agreed on about how we should respond to what we describe under the general heading of complex or wide-scale abuse investigations. It's a strange heading, but never mind about that. It includes historical abuse allegations in schools, so what we are dealing with from you clearly falls within that.'

He spluttered on, thinking on his feet and clearly not prepared. 'Our role in social services, however, is more limited than you might have thought. There is an issue about what our appropriate role is. You are obviously asking for clarification on that in your last letter because you have specifically said "can the DE confirm that I have the authority to investigate the LEA?" Frankly, to be honest with you, I'm not sure that I have got that authority. What the DE has done is to send that letter of yours to my boss and to me saying could we advise him on a response. So that is what's going on at this moment. Perhaps I shouldn't pre-empt this, but it's my view that it is not within my authority to do that.'

I asked him to explain what the terms of reference for the inquiry were. He said that they would liaise with the police about any information they already had and what investigations they could make. Their aim was to have a coordinated response with the police. He added that given the fact that I was an adult, and they were not aware at that stage of any current child protection issues in connection with my former teacher, although there may be some, that it would be mainly a police led investigation. He concluded by saying that he did not yet know the name of the teacher, so I told him the name and how to spell it, and thanked him for his time.

The next day, my MP's secretary called me to ask if I had had a reply from the Director of Education. I said that I had, and I explained where things stood. She asked if I wanted a reply from the Secretary of State. I said that as long as he was aware of my case, that was OK. She said that he was aware, wished me luck and said goodbye.

Later that day, I wrote to the head of the Child Protection Unit, following up our earlier conversation. I enclosed a copy of my original testimony and copies of the letters and my school reports. It was obvious from the Director of Education's response to my first letter to him that this was the first he had known about my case, yet the school had been contacted about it by my solicitor in September 1999. This would indicate that the LEA had not been informed by the school that an investigation was underway. Although the school had been an independent Church school when I first went there, it was later taken over by the LEA. I said this worried me as it was a repeat of what had happened in 1968 when I first informed them. I told him that I was deeply sceptical about the way inquiries are conducted, and that I was adamant that this time those actually responsible for what happened to me would be identified, challenged and dealt with appropriately.

A week later, he sent me a copy of their procedures for investigating child abuse cases. The document was very wordy and certainly gave the appearance that child abuse was being taken seriously by local authorities. It stated that their general principles were to ensure that any necessary action is taken to secure the immediate safety of children, that the needs of the children concerned were paramount, and should inform the manner and timing of the investigation, and, subject to the requirements of full investigation and any necessary action, disruption to the establishment concerned would be kept to a minimum. It went on and on about how the relevant agencies would cooperate in assessing what was required, and that they would all work together, pooling resources where appropriate, to meet the diverse needs of individual children and groups of children ... etc ... etc ... etc.

Despite the long-winded jargon most of the document contained, it ended with this unambiguous statement, which was encouraging. 'It is of the greatest importance that those in authority are clear that, although there may be insufficient evidence to support a police prosecution, this does not mean that action does not need to be taken to protect the child, or that disciplinary procedures should not be invoked and pursued.' Maybe the bureaucrats really had learnt the lessons of the past.

On 14 February, I received a letter from the head of the Pupil Support and Independent Schools Division at the Department for Education and Employment. It appeared that the letter I had sent to the Secretary of State really had been read by the man himself. The letter said how very sorry they were to read about my experiences at school, and they wanted to assure me the Government was concerned that children should be protected from abuse. Enclosed with the letter was a copy of the department's child protection guidance circular entitled 'Protecting Children from Abuse: The Role of the Education Service'. It set out the action to be taken by teachers with designated responsibility for child abuse issues, where there are suspicions that a child may be at risk from abuse. It included advice on what action should be taken if teachers or other members of staff were themselves accused of abuse. Also enclosed were two other circulars entitled 'Working Together for the Protection of Children from Abuse: Procedures within the Education Service', and 'Working Together to Safeguard Children', a guide to inter-agency working to safeguard and promote the welfare of children.

Then, as if by way of excusing what had happened, the letter said, 'Unfortunately, these policies were not in existence when you were at school.' You must be joking, I thought. What possible difference would they have made? They are certainly not making any difference today. Don't they read the press? Hardly a week goes by without the courts dealing with sexual abuse in schools.

Like Pontius Pilate washing his hands as he handed Christ to be crucified, the letter concluded by saying, 'I have been assured by the Local Education Authority that all schools in the Authority, and the Authority itself, now have child protection policies which reflect the advice contained in our Circular 10/95, and the procedures set out by the local Area Child Protection Committee. I understand from them, that the child protection procedures are currently being revised and that they would be more than happy to let you see a copy in draft.' Oh, well, that's all right then. We can sleep safe in our beds in the sure knowledge that all the little children are safe. What they did not know was that at the same time that they were writing to me, at the primary school where my wife was teaching, a young male student teacher was abusing some of the children in her class. He was later arrested, prosecuted and convicted after one of the boys told his mother.

The school's head had been aware of concerns about the student expressed by my wife and other teachers who had observed his unusual fondness for the children, but she had dismissed their concerns and done nothing. So much for their policies. In my mind I had a vision of hundreds of bureaucrats, their heads in the sand, surrounded by piles of unread copies of their child protection policies, while in the background the voices of little children went unheard.

Telling them that they were living in cloud-cuckoo-land would not have helped my campaign, so, a few days later, I replied saying that I was greatly encouraged by the response I had had from the LEA and now from them. I wanted them to know that there was much still to be done, and while I was grateful for their assurances, I wanted them to know how difficult it was to resurrect the awful memories associated with this dreadful period of my life, but it had to be done if I was ever going to recover and begin to help other victims of abuse. I confirmed that I was fully prepared to go through with what I had begun, regardless of how unpleasant it might get.

On 22 February, the LEA's Service Coordinator wrote to tell me that she was now responsible for coordinating the investigation into my allegation of abuse, and to ensure that any outstanding child protection issues were identified and properly dealt with. She explained the process, saying that it would begin with a strategy meeting, attended by Social Services, the police, a representative from the County Council Education Department and a representative from the school. The meeting would hear the details of my allegations, any action taken to date, and plan the action required to investigate fully. It would also examine as far as possible whether my allegations gave rise to any current child protection concerns, and if so how these would be addressed. She said she would contact me again following the meeting to explain the planned course of action. It was a wonderful feeling. I had stuck a large stick in their ant hill and all the ants were running around like crazy trying to fix it up! Things had come a long, long way since Sealy had said, 'They won't believe you.'

The following day Susan e-mailed saying she had completed my statement and she would like me to come down and go through it with her. Two days later, the Director of Education at the County Council wrote saying that the Child Protection and Independent Review Unit of the Social Services Department was convening a meeting to plan an investigation into the allegations I had made. He said that the LEA would be represented at that meeting and they would have to agree how to investigate the issues I had raised that would not be covered by the joint inquiry led by Social Services and the police. Only after that discussion had occurred on 3 March could they make a decision about how to manage any enquiries which fell outside the main investigation.

He finished by saying that both the Social Services Department and the police had the authority to investigate an inquiry into all aspects of the allegations, including the previous involvement of his department with my school. 'The Education Department will co-operate fully in this matter. There are complicating factors which the LEA will have to consider. The first relates to the legal status of the School, and the second to the length of time since the alleged events took place. Any records held by the LEA will be made available to Social Services and the Police.'

On 8 March, I drove down to the police station and went through the nine-page typed statement with Susan. I made some minor amendments to the spelling of names. Reading the statement for the first time since I had made it back in November shocked me as it was so real. There in front of me in cold print was the full account of what had happened, in all its awful detail. I found it very disturbing and we spent some time talking about the whole subject and what was still to come. Susan was very understanding and made me feel very much at ease. She updated me on the outcome of the strategy meeting that took place on 3 March, then paused for a moment before saying that Sealy was still alive. In fact, he had only recently retired from teaching – it was at another school run by the same organisation that taught me. She said she had also found my old headmaster.

'He's also alive and living in a nursing home. He's said to be a bit doddery, but I and a colleague intend to visit him soon. We will also be paying a visit to both schools.' The 'specialist' who came to interrogate me had also been identified. There was now no going back, no recoiling from the demons I had unlocked, the bus to freedom was really moving now.

On 7 April, Susan phoned to say she had been to see the head teacher at Sealy's last school and got all of his details.

'I have also been to see your old headmaster at the nursing home. He was very helpful, well, I say helpful, but he couldn't remember anything! He made out that he was giving us all the help he could, but then having said that he couldn't remember anything about what I wanted to speak to him about. Basically he has provided what we call a negative statement, i.e. saying I've been asked about this but I can't remember anything at all! So that's that.'

Susan's next words made the hair on the back of my neck stand up.

'There are some things of concern that have come up from the other school that we may need to look into. It would appear Sealy had some sort of liaisons with pupils while he was there, but there were never any allegations, or any concern that he was being inappropriate. That is something we will follow up aside from your allegations. So the next thing is that I will write to Mr Sealy and invite him in for interview. I would imagine he has heard through the grapevine what is going on already.' She added that she was quite surprised that he had not been in touch already.

'I don't know about you, but I would want to know what is being said. It appears that they moved him to the other school when you left. He's been there ever since, but interestingly there is nothing in his personnel file about anything to do with you. But then you don't know if it was swept under the carpet in those days or what, do you? I mean nowadays, God, it should be logged so carefully and there is nothing in that file, not even an explanation as to why he moved from one school to the other. You have to wonder about that as he wasn't at your school for very long, a bit more than a year maybe. The rest of his career was spent at the other school. The fact that he moved there shortly after you left is very interesting! I'll let you know how I get on with our Mr Sealy.' I thanked her for everything she had done and put the phone down. I felt sick. My hands started to shake as I wrote down a note of what she had said for my record.

On 2 May, Susan phoned again to let me know that she had arrested Sealy the week before! I was almost dumbfounded at the news.

'Yes, a bit of a shock out of the blue for you!' she said. 'I wrote him a little letter and he came on down with his solicitor to the police station, where I arrested him. We didn't get very far though because, although he was deemed fit to be interviewed by our people, his solicitor put up a bit of a fight saying he wasn't fit to be interviewed because he wasn't feeling too well. He certainly didn't look well after I started to interview him!'

Susan said she had bailed him to reattend in a fortnight, when she would 'have another go' at interviewing him.

'At the end of the day,' she said, 'he needs to be given a chance to answer the allegations.' I asked her if he looked anything like he did in the school photo?

'No,' she replied, 'he is very grey and obviously a lot older. He's a wizened old man really. I'm away next week so I'll have another go the following Wednesday – two weeks tomorrow – I'll try to interview him again then. I'll call you afterwards.'

I put the phone down, punched the air with my fists and shouted out loud: 'Yes – yes – yes – how did you like that then Sealy, you bastard?'

9

Justice denied

Susan phoned again on 18 May. It was not the news I'd prayed for, but it was what I'd half expected.

'Hello, Peter. Well, Mr Sealy came along yesterday with his solicitor and we eventually interviewed him. Do you know what I am going to say next?'

'You are either going to say he denied it, or he coughed.'

'Which one do you reckon?'

'I'd like to reckon that he coughed, but I think he probably denied it.'

'Yes, that's right, but, spookily enough, a lot of the details you gave in your statement he agreed with, i.e. the trip to Wales, the home tutoring, that sort of thing, but none of the offences. He agreed with everything, but not the offences.'

'At least his memory still works.'

'Well, when it suits him it does. So, basically we've got your word against his, which we thought would be the case anyway. So what I've done is bailed him for six weeks and I'll be submitting an advice file to the CPS, which is the way you thought it would go.'

'Yes, that's wonderful, thank you.'

'That's all right. It could take longer than six weeks to be honest, but as soon as I know what's happening I'll let you know. I got your consent forms through so I think I'll send them off and get copies of your medical notes.'

'Thank you for all your help so far.'

'That's all right – no problem. It is moving, isn't it?'

'Yes.'

'What about if they say no, it isn't going to go to court?'

'I'm prepared for that. I would simply proceed with the private prosecution.'

'Sure.'

'It's not going to go away, that's the thing.'

'That's right. The bloke's a wreck, though, I have to say. It should make you feel a bit better to know that this thing has stressed him out no end and he's lost a lot of weight since he came in last time. He is worried!'

On 8 May, the LEA's Service Coordinator wrote informing me that they had not been able to hold the meeting they had planned for 5 May due to the police being unable to attend. They had rescheduled the meeting for 25 May and would be in contact with me again after then. I heard no more until 27 June when they wrote to say that there had been no further allegations made against Sealy to date, and, consequently, they were waiting for the decision of the Crown Prosecution Service as to whether they would proceed with my case into court. They would then decide what further work should be undertaken in order to respond to my allegations.

A week later, on 3 July, Susan rang with the news we had all been waiting for. It was the worst news in the world. She said she had received a reply from the CPS following the file she had submitted to them. It said they had carefully considered the allegations I had made but, as the police had not been able to corroborate my allegations, plus the fact that the teacher I had confided in had died, and that my old headmaster, Mr Smith, did not recall any such allegations being made to him, they were left simply with my evidence, which Sealy denied. Consequently, they said, they regretted that, in the circumstances, they could not see that there was a realistic prospect of conviction in this case and, accordingly, could not advise any proceedings being instituted against Sealy.

So, after everything I had been through, I was to be denied even the opportunity to challenge in court the man who had destroyed me. I felt completely numb. He had got away with it again. I asked Susan if that was the end of the road from a police point of view. She said that the file would remain with them and that my statement still stood. If something did happen further down the line, such as another witness coming forward, they would resurrect the case. However, the file would only be held there, it would not appear on the national police computer because Sealy had not been convicted, so if another witness came forward in another part of the country, my allegations would not flash up when they searched the system.

I could tell from Susan's voice that she was as gutted as I was. She had put so much effort into the investigation and it had all come to nothing. I thanked her again for everything she had done and told her that I couldn't really have got this far without her help. She wished me good luck for the future and we said goodbye. My guardian angel had gone. I was back to square one, alone, confused and angry. I could see him smirking. Oh, how I hated him.

On 11 July, the Head of Education Children's Services wrote to me to say that they had carried out a detailed investigation of all their historic records to see if there was anything from my school relating to me. They had found nothing and were, regrettably, unable to progress the matter further. On 31 July, I received another letter from Social Services saying that no further work could be undertaken to investigate my allegations now that the police investigation had stopped. I felt so low. The elation I had experienced when Susan told me she had arrested Sealy had evaporated as, one by one, the avenues I had explored in my search for justice had turned into dead ends. I closed my study door and went for a long walk with my faithful dog, Emma. She wouldn't let me down, nor I her.

A week went by and, gradually, a new sense of purpose began to fill my mind. I was calmer now and not so despairing. The anger inside had once again gone cold, but it had not gone away. If anything, its flame was burning brighter. I decided there was still one more thing I could do to keep my fight going. I would challenge the CPS decision. So, on 7 August, I wrote to the CPS branch that dealt with my case and asked them to explain in detail why they had denied me the chance to bring my case before a judge and jury; after all, there must be dozens of cases tried by the courts every day that do not end with a conviction. Why were those cases able to go before the courts, but not mine?

On 14 August, I received a reply from the Chief Crown Prosecutor herself. At least they were taking my complaint seriously, I thought when I opened the letter and saw her name on the bottom. I read it carefully, and then read it again. The detailed explanation I had asked for was exactly what I got, but it did not help me. Sealy had escaped because the law, as it is written, says the defendant is more important than the victim. At least, that's the way it seemed.

The basis of their decision was that, in view of the passage of time, they would be unable to satisfy a jury to the required standard that the offences had been committed in the way that I had described, and, further, that in any event the judge would in all likelihood refuse to allow the matter to proceed on the basis that Sealy could not have a fair trial. It was an abuse of the criminal process to prosecute offenders where they have been denied that basic right of a fair trial. This means that they have to be in a position to defend themselves against the allegation.

'You will appreciate,' she said, 'that over 30 years have passed, and that this is the first time Mr Sealy has been faced with these allegations. Clearly, he is not in a position to put forward an effective defence. I appreciate that you, as a victim, also have rights but the Crown Prosecution Service acts in the public interest in prosecuting rather than the interests of one individual. It would be wholly wrong to put this matter before the court in the full knowledge that, even if the Judge allowed the matter to proceed, we could not satisfy any jury to the very high standard required before they could find Mr Sealy guilty.'

So then, as far as the criminal law was concerned, unless other victims came forward, that was the end of the matter. Sealy had escaped justice and was free to continue, unchallenged, to abuse, violate and blight the lives of more young boys. God only knows how many others he had already done that to. The anger and frustration inside me grew again. I could not and would not let it end here.

10

And all the world shall know

I still felt desperately lonely. I had nothing really to show for all I had been through, save the satisfaction of knowing that Sealy had at least suffered the humiliation of being arrested and questioned after all these years. I was adamant that he was not going to beat me. I would find other victims, but to do that I would first have to tell the rest of the world what had happened to me.

Summer was beginning to fade. It was almost a year since I had written my original account of what had happened. On a bright September morning I went into my study and collected together all of the documents and correspondence I had received from everyone involved so far, including the old letters from school that my father had given me. I put them all into chronological order and began to scan them into my computer. I added all of the letters I had written, my medical notes and the original document I had written for Allan. I then wrote an introduction to it all, and placed the entire archive on a web site I had registered under the domain name Victims No Longer. I was now ready. If Sealy had thought it was over, he was very wrong. It had only just begun. The little boy he had abused and betrayed all those years ago was now a man. I was no longer frightened of what he could do, or what anyone else could do for that matter. I was going to tell my story to the world, and they were just going to have to deal with the consequences.

On 6 September, I wrote once more to the Director of Education, the head of the CPS, the police and the Secretary of State for Education, to inform them of my plans. I told them that I had asked my solicitor to file a claim in the High Court against Sealy and the school, and that I had written a full account of what happened and placed it on a web site, which, subject to approval from my solicitor, would be linked to the major search engines and thus be available for the world to view at will.

I told them that the purpose of the site was threefold: to help other victims of abuse find the courage to tell of their ordeals and begin the painful and difficult process of recovery; to help them understand the difficulties they could expect to face when they do inform the authorities; and to find the other victims that Sealy had abused so that a successful criminal case could be brought against him, bringing an end to his reign of terror and allowing all the lost souls he had destroyed to live once more as men. I signed the letters Peter Andrews – Victim No Longer.

I discussed the plan with Allan, who advised that, for the time being, I should not refer to Sealy by his real name on the web site. I could live with that, so I deleted all the references to him, replacing them with the letter X. Having done that, I sent an e-mail to the various search engines with the details of the site. Victims No Longer would become visible for all the world to see in a matter of hours. I had told them all that I would do it, and now I had.

But there remained one more thing to do: to tell my children what I had done and why. Up to this point, none of them knew anything about what had happened, they only knew that I had been ill. William was 20, Elizabeth 17½, and Thomas just 16. Not surprisingly, each took my bombshell revelation in different ways. But, once the initial shock had worn off, they were glad I had told them, and they swore that if I didn't 'nail the bastard', they would do it for me!

It was not an easy decision to tell them, but the thought of them hearing about it from someone other than me was just not in the running. As a parent, I felt I had no real choice but to tell them, and their reactions told me that I had done the right thing. It was time to release the hounds.

Within hours of the web site going live, I received an e-mail from another pupil at the school that stunned me. He said that he too had been abused, but not by Sealy. He also talked of a cover-up, saying he had witnessed a regime of abuse perpetrated by a small minority which was ignored by the school authorities.

'On the one occasion I was a victim,' he said, 'I rationalised it by saying that it was probably my fault anyway, and that I had deserved the "punishment". Telling my parents I had been molested in a shower would have driven a fault line through their unquestioning faith in the integrity of institutions.'

Over the next few days, I received many more messages of support, one of which seemed to hold a vital clue. The message talked about sexual abuse by one of the teachers at the school, but did not name him. I replied several times, asking the contact to tell me the teacher's name. The contact refused each time saying that he just couldn't face the thought of his family, now grown up like mine, finding out about it. He was desperately sorry, but he just couldn't risk it.

A week went by and I'd heard no more from this man. Then, one afternoon, as I sat at my desk wondering what to do next, 'YOU HAVE E-MAIL' popped up on the screen.

'I've changed my mind,' the message said. 'I will tell you who it was, but you have to promise not to involve me. It was Mr Swanson who abused me.' I felt physically sick and my heart began to race. Mr Swanson was, of course, the very same teacher I had confided in.

Allan had made an appointment for us both to meet a barrister who, he had been told, was experienced in dealing with child abuse cases. So, armed with my latest 'clue', off we went to see him. He was not what I had expected. He had little if any understanding of the impact of childhood sexual abuse on males. He even doubted that the mental breakdown I had suffered recently was in fact PTSD. I was annoyed by his compromising attitude so I asked him if he had any experience in cases involving psycho-sexual trauma. He was clearly uncomfortable at the question, not because he couldn't give me a positive answer, but simply because I had dared to ask him such a question.

I was not impressed by this man and wanted to leave. The clincher was when he said it would cost about £50,000 to bring a case to court, and in his view, I had a less than 30 per cent chance of success. Even if I did win, the damages would be modest. I thanked him for his time, and we left. On the way home, I told Allan that I would do it on my own.

'What, act for yourself?'

'Yes. I am just as capable of screwing the case up as he is, but for a fraction of the cost!' We both laughed.

After a brief pause, Allan said: 'You're serious, aren't you?

'You'd better believe it', I replied. 'Deadly, bloody serious.'

The following day was 20 October, my birthday. I was 49 years old. What better day to begin the next stage in my fight for justice? I took a deep breath and plunged right in, writing to the solicitors acting for the school, advising them that I was now acting as litigant in person, and that they should correspond directly with me from now on. I told them that I intended to sue them and Sealy, and that I would be filing a claim for damages in the High Court as soon as I had completed the documentation. I also added that I had now received testimonies from two other pupils at my school who stated that they had been sexually abused by Mr Swanson. I sent a copy to the headmaster of the school Sealy had been moved to, and a copy to the current headmaster of my old school.

Two days later, the school's solicitors replied. It was a very different response to the original, dismissive letter they had sent Allan all those months ago. They asked if I could give them a little more time, but implored me not to think that they were trying to be anything other than very concerned. They took the matter very seriously, but in light of recent developments, they would need to speak in some detail with their client. They also assured me that I should not be concerned if the heads of the two schools did not reply to my letters directly. All correspondence would be dealt with by them. At long last, I had managed to find and press their 'panic' button, so I wrote to them again, asking for the names and addresses of all involved so I could write to them individually to ask them to provide witness statements. I was not the least bit fearful of them and I was certainly not going to let them intimidate me again.

On 3 November they replied, asking for yet more time as they were now 'taking instructions on all the issues' I had raised. They again assured me that everyone was taking the matter 'very seriously'.

However, unbeknown to me at the time, there were other dark forces at work in the background.

That evening, I logged on to my web site to check the e-mail. The message on my screen said simply: 'ACCESS DENIED'. I tried again. 'ACCESS DENIED'. I sent a quick e-mail to the web site host asking if the system was down.

'We have been ordered to shut down your site,' came the reply.

'By whom?' I asked.

'A teachers' union.' So, even though I hadn't named him on the site, Sealy had gone to his union and asked them to protect him. I was now up against a very powerful force. It was time to take the gloves off.

The following morning, I rang the regional office of the union that served the area where Sealy had last worked. Eventually, after the usual run-around you get from an unsolicited phone call, I was put through to the Regional Director. I asked him if he had shut down my site – 'yes or no?' He wasn't willing at first to tell me anything. I explained a bit more about what Sealy had actually done to me and asked him how he would feel if Sealy's next victim was his son? Eventually, he confirmed that they had taken the action on behalf of one of their members after receiving a request from the member, who 'has not been charged, let alone convicted, with any offence'. If I wanted to take the matter further, I should write to the union's head office.

That afternoon, I wrote to the then General Secretary of the union, asking him why he had shut down my site. He did not reply. I wrote to him several more times, but still got no reply. The union's actions in closing down my web site, coupled with their silence, made me feel abused all over again. It also showed that all those fine words sent to me by the DFEE and the County Council about how they have tightened up their child protection procedures was no more than hot air. I thought back to something the barrister had said to me: 'You could always name him and let him sue you for libel. He probably wouldn't want to, though, as it would be far more of a risk for him than it would be for you!'

That was the answer – I would do just that. I contacted my internet service provider and asked if they provided any space on their server for private home pages. Yes, they did. Within hours, everything I had put on my original site was back on the internet! Only this time, I had identified Sealy by his full name.

Over the next few days, I e-mailed as many people as I could think of with the web site address asking for anyone who had any information about Sealy to contact me. More information came through, although not about Sealy specifically, but I passed it all on to the police anyway.

The site remained up for ten days before Sealy's union contacted my internet service provider and threatened them with unspecified action unless they took the site down. However, neither the union nor Sealy were threatening any action against me, so the barrister had been right. In a way, I didn't mind now as I'd got more than enough people to look at the site. Everyone who needed to know did know. The site was duly shut down, reluctantly, by the ISP, who told me that they were very sorry to have to close my site, but as it contained material that infringed their own policies, they had no choice. They said that they were doing so with a heavy heart, but wished me luck! Who said the corporate world had no room for people's feelings?

The time had come to concentrate my efforts on the legal case but, with no real knowledge of the law, I was going to have to go back to school. I went to my local library and borrowed all the books they had about civil law and criminal law. I read and read until I could read no more, and by the end of November, I had finished preparing a formal statement of claim using the format shown in the law books. I sent a copy of this to the school's solicitors, with an outline of my case, explaining what I was going to sue their client for, and why.

On 29 November they replied, saying that they had had a meeting with representatives of their client at which they had considered my letters.

'Our client now needs a little more time to consider further some ideas for a constructive approach to resolving the issues you have raised. The purpose of writing at the moment is to assure you that our client has matters under active consideration. We hope to be in a position to come back to you substantively before very much longer, and appreciate your patience.'

It was just over a year since the first, dismissive contact with them. Finally, it looked as though they were going to make a move. I was drained and exhausted, but happy.

11

The reckoning

December has always been a special time of the year in our family. It is a time of giving, a time of hope and celebration. How apt then that it was December when the school's solicitors offered their olive branch, spurred on perhaps by the knowledge that I intended to file my claim against them in the High Court any day.

The content of their letter was both unexpected and hard to believe. I read it several times just to be sure I was not dreaming. They said they had now received instructions from their client and were writing to set out a way forward. Their proposal was for the school and me to endeavour to resolve the issues between us through a process of formal mediation administered by an independent body. They said the mediation process was very simple and very speedy.

'It might be possible to produce an outcome by, say, the end of February. Our client would be represented at the mediation by someone who had authority to enter into a final and binding resolution of the issues between you and the school. We look forward to hearing from you with what we hope will be a positive response.'

I almost went into shock. What they were really saying was that they did not want to get anywhere near a courtroom, preferring to settle the matter out of court. After all this time and energy, the end was in sight. I showed the letter to my wife Anne, and then to each of my children in turn. They all agreed it would be a good idea to try. I mulled it over for several hours, trying to work out why the school authorities were now so keen to settle the matter.

Maybe they had found out that there were other victims, maybe their solicitors had told them I was not going to go away? No matter how hard I thought about it, I couldn't come up with a solution that was anything more than guesswork. There were simply too many different scenarios and possibilities. The only way to find out was to sit down round the table and hear what they had to say, so the following day I faxed them a letter confirming my agreement to the mediation.

From then on, events began to move swiftly. A firm of London-based mediators were appointed and a date for the hearing was fixed for 12 February, 2001. I began to feel very anxious. After all this time, all the denials, all the setbacks, suddenly they wanted to talk. Was it a trap? Were they just trying to put more pressure on me in the hope that I would go away?

Over the next few days, my resolve began to harden and I started to write out what I would say on the day, but the more I wrote, the more I realised that I couldn't do it on my own. What if I broke down? What if I just couldn't face it once it got underway? I realised I would have to ask someone I could trust to come with me. I would ask Michael Brown, someone I had met along my journey, a kind and intelligent man who knew all about the management of vulnerability.

Michael had become a close friend in a very short space of time. I first met him when I went to work at the psychiatric hospital in 1996. He was the only member of the hospital's senior management whom I had come to trust during those terrible months of the judicial inquiry. He was well aware of what I was going through as, for different reasons, he too was going through his own psychological trauma as a result of the fallout of the inquiry. It was this mutual bond of understanding between us that had cemented our friendship, but whether he would want to involve himself in even more trauma was something I could not just take for granted. I would have to give him the opportunity to say no without him feeling bad about that.

To my relief, he said yes as soon as I asked him. Immediately I began to feel much more positive and a lot less fearful. Michael had many years of experience working with vulnerable children and adults on both sides of the divide – victims and offenders. He understood every aspect of child protection issues and had little time for those who tried to protect abusers at the expense of their victims. He would prove invaluable.

Over the next couple of weeks, I wrote several times more to the General Secretary of Sealy's union, asking for a response to my previous letters. I got none, but rather than continue to challenge him, I decided to put everything on hold so that my family could enjoy a happy Christmas. It was not until I had shut my study door that I realised just how exhausted I was and how remote I had become from the day-to-day life which was going on around me. The break was a wonderful release from it all and it was for me the best Christmas in many a year.

Once the new year had begun, it was time to get back into the fight. I felt regenerated and fired up for what lay ahead. I spent the next three weeks preparing my case summary for the mediators. When I'd completed it, the time had come to tell my abuser what was about to happen. I'd got his address from a colleague who worked in the press. He had a CD with the complete UK electoral register on it! It took him a matter of seconds to find Sealy's address. It was the same house he had taken me to all those years ago.

With a mixture of trepidation and anticipation, I wrote to Sealy, telling him in very matter-of-fact terms that I would be meeting representatives from his former employer in February to discuss my claim for damages against them. I added that, depending on the outcome of that meeting, I may agree to drop my claim against the school, but regardless of the outcome, 'I will still file a claim for compensatory, aggravated and exemplary damages against you for the terrible things you did to me when I was a child.' Of all the letters I had written so far, this one was the most satisfying, and I read it out loud to myself several times before I signed it and sealed the envelope.

A week before we were due to meet, I received a copy of the school's case summary, which had been written by their solicitors. When I'd finished reading it, I knew in my heart that all the words of assurance I had been given over the past months by the Local Authority, the Education Department and Social Services were of little use. In reality, we were no further forward now than we were 30 years ago when I was abused. They had all talked about listening to the child, believing the child, and being able to protect victims of abuse through their better understanding of the issues. In practice, as the school's case summary demonstrated, the reality is that victims still have to prove they were abused before anyone takes any notice. Unless they can do that, they face a very steep hill to climb and, of course, as the statistics show, many simply can't face the struggle and they end their own lives.

The school's document talked about the 'burden' on Mr Andrews to prove that I had been abused. They said that they did not accept that the illness I had suffered was in any way connected, and that I should have raised the issue long before now.

'Mr Andrews was well aware that what he alleges was happening to him was wrong, and he had three years from reaching the age of 18 in which to bring a claim.'

They also said that I would have to overcome the hurdle of proving that my case was factually correct.

'In this respect, the matter would primarily be one of his word against Mr Sealy's. In this context it is a matter of concern to the school that at the outset of Mr Andrews' complaint, he had difficulty in remembering the name of his teacher.'

Their final insult was to say that I would have to show that I was entitled to compensation.

'There can be a large number of reasons why pupils do not succeed in examinations and the fact that Mr Andrews succeeded five years later in three papers does not mean that he was failed by the school at the age of 16. The passage of time increases maturity, and changing circumstances can increase motivation.' This was a reference to the fact that when I was 21, I went to night school for a year to study three GCE O levels, which I subsequently passed.

Their position was one of total denial, yet they wanted to mediate! It was a joke. They simply wanted to get rid of me as quickly and as cheaply as possible, with the minimum of publicity into the bargain. They even denied that Mr Swanson had been wrong to use our conversation against me.

They argued that it was by no means uncommon to ask someone who had confided in someone in authority to allow that person to repeat matters shared in confidence with others who might be in a position to help. If Mr Swanson had insisted on keeping my confidence, my complaints would never have been heard at all. The school, so they said, believed that Mr Swanson had behaved entirely properly if he encouraged me to disclose what had happened to me.

Having made their bold-faced denials that they were in any way responsible for what had happened, they concluded their summary by saying that they would 'listen sympathetically to as much as Mr Andrews wishes to add in person at the mediation. The school's representatives will then do all they can to work constructively towards a solution which repairs the damage to Mr Andrews' quality of life which he claims he suffered. The school will consider whether, in the light of all available information, it would be right to acknowledge in appropriate terms that it did not respond appropriately to matters raised by Mr Andrews, and whether it can assist Mr Andrews financially in continuing the process of healing and recovery upon which he has embarked.'

Although I had already written and submitted my case summary, I decided that I had to respond to the crap they had put down as their defence. I wrote back to the mediators and challenged the school's 'position' as forcefully as I could. They were not going to walk over me. I was no longer a frightened child and I didn't care about keeping my story out of the news; on the contrary, I wanted everyone to know exactly what these people had done to me, and no doubt to many others besides.

Two days later, I received a letter from another firm of solicitors, acting on Sealy's behalf. With pompous indignation, they threatened vigorously to defend any action I might take against their client. They even went as far as saying that my actions thus far had resulted in their client 'suffering with extreme anxiety and stress which has had an adverse effect on his health'.

If I were to sue Sealy, they said, 'not only will he defend your action, but will also counterclaim against you in your own action, seeking damages and compensation as well as an order for costs'.

I read the letter over and over. If this was the best he could do to frighten me off, it was a pretty pathetic effort. So, he was suffering from extreme anxiety and stress was he? Good, let me make it even more uncomfortable! I wrote back the same day saying that I was not surprised that their client maintained his denial.

'After all, he is looking at a ten-year custodial sentence if convicted. He is therefore hardly likely to willingly admit to the offence is he?' As for the distress he was claiming to have suffered as a result of my disclosure, well, talk about taking the piss, the cheeky git. I ended my letter by saying perhaps he should have thought a little harder about the possible consequences of his actions before he abused and raped me.

'Spit the bones out of that, you bastard,' I said to myself, as I pushed the letter into the postbox.

12

Judgement day

I didn't sleep at all for the next few nights. A million thoughts kept surging through my mind. I wanted it to be over, but I also wanted it to happen. I had spent the past 12 months, day in, day out, preparing for this moment, but when the day finally came, I felt very exposed and unprepared. Although the hearing was not in a courtroom, it was still me against them. I had to be strong. If I weakened, they would crush me. This was a serious business for everyone; they knew it and I knew it.

Michael picked me up early in the morning and drove me to the place chosen for the mediation. It was a neutral location, miles from either of us. The week before, I had also asked Allan if he would join us on the day just in case they tried to outmanoeuvre me with legal arguments that I didn't understand. He was waiting for us when we arrived. I can't tell you just how much strength it gave me to see him there. Once inside, we were shown to a room and asked to wait. Tea and coffee were already in the room. I poured a cup for each of us and we chatted about nothing in particular.

After about ten minutes, a woman in her fifties appeared with a man in his thirties. The woman introduced herself as the mediator and her colleague as her assistant. She appeared confident and friendly, her colleague more anxious and less talkative. I introduced myself, Michael and Allan, and, after the usual pleasantries and comments about the weather had been exchanged, she explained that the process we were about to engage in would involve a meeting alone with her first, then a joint meeting, then a break for lunch and, finally, a further joint meeting at which, hopefully, a resolution and agreement would be reached. She also said that during the various sessions, she would refer to each of us by our first names to make the discussions more friendly.

By 11 a.m. we had finished our meeting with the mediator. It was now time to meet the other side. I was dreading it. I was about to step back 30 years and look into the eyes of those who'd betrayed me all that time ago. I felt like running away, but I knew I had to go into that room. After all this time, I had brought the school authorities back to the table to ask them: 'Do you believe me now?'

The mediator went in first, followed by Allan, Michael and then I. At the table sat two men, one old, the other a little younger. A tall man, their solicitor, sat next to them. The mediator introduced us all to each other and we sat down, on opposite sides of the large, rectangular oak table. Michael had earlier agreed with the mediator that he would present the opening statement on my behalf. The mediator brought the meeting to order and we began.

'Michael,' she said. 'Please would you like to begin with your opening.'

'Could I ask that we begin with a prayer?' I interjected politely. There was a stunned silence, then the older one said: 'Yes. I think that would be a good thing to do.' We lowered our heads and he began to recite the prayer that is perhaps the best-known prayer on the planet, the Lord's Prayer:

> Our Father, who art in heaven, hallowed be thy Name; thy kingdom come; thy will be done; on earth as it is in heaven. Give us this day our daily bread. And forgive us our trespasses, as we forgive those who trespass against us. And lead us not into temptation;

but deliver us from evil. For thine is the kingdom, the power, and the glory, for ever and ever. Amen.

The Methodist Worship Book
© Trustees for Methodist
Church Purposes, 1999

It was, in every sense, the only prayer he could have said.

Michael picked up his piece of paper and began to speak.

'My name is Michael Brown. I am a close friend of Peter and his family, yet I have known him for just four years. In that relatively short time, however, I have come to know him very well. In 1996, Peter was employed by my Chief Executive to advise the Board of our hospital in relation to a number of highly sensitive issues that were about to be brought into the media spotlight. His experience in media relations was extremely helpful to us, so much so, that when, a year later, we were faced with an inquiry into allegations of child abuse and other issues, he stayed on under my direct supervision as a trusted member of our team.

'It was as a result of the challenges and pressures we faced together in carrying out this difficult and harrowing task that we developed a very close professional bond based on trust, mutual respect and understanding of the issues involved, and it was as a result of this bond that Peter turned to me for help as a friend when, in 1998, his own difficulties began to overwhelm him. It is as his friend that I stand here before you today and speak on his behalf.

'We have all read Peter's case summary and I do not therefore propose to go over it again in any detail. However, what I do want to do is offer some observations and thoughts for consideration as we conduct this process of mediation in an attempt to settle this matter to the benefit of all parties.

'Firstly, let me address the issue of the truth and credibility of children and young people. In my experience as a social worker dealing with the many damaged, abused and betrayed children, young people and adults whom I have worked with over the years, I can say without hesitation that when a child or a young person in crisis tells you that they are being abused, they are invariably telling the truth.

'When Peter confided in Mr Swanson, and then the school authorities, back in the autumn of 1967, he was only just 16 – a minor; frightened, confused and clearly in crisis. Just thinking about the mental anguish he must have gone through in making the decision to disclose what was happening to him is made all the worse when we consider that he did not do it to cause trouble. He did not do it out of spite or a misguided sense of vengeance. He did not do it to empower himself in the eyes of his peers. He did it because he wanted to spare the family of his friend Simon the pain of watching him not take part with them in Simon's funeral service. This act of sacrifice, for that is what it was – he sacrificed the safety of keeping his awful secrets for the unknown consequences of telling all – to help lessen the pain of Simon's parents, brother and sisters, in their time of tragedy, was a remarkable thing to have done.

'The circumstances of Peter's disclosure, however, I find deeply disturbing. As I understand things, respecting someone's need for their confidence to be kept is vital for those who care for others and children in particular. Yet in this case, Peter's secrets were not kept secret, and, if that were not bad enough, they were then used against him by the school. Given that there was no positive outcome for Peter from all this, it is difficult to come up with any justification for Mr Swanson's actions at the time of the conversation, or the headmaster's subsequent actions when he was told the details of Peter's conversation with Mr Swanson.

'More recently, however, another former pupil at the school has come forward and said that he and two other boys were "sexually molested" by Mr Swanson in the shower after a cross-country run. They were all only 13 years old at the time. Another former pupil has testified that he was physically assaulted by Mr Swanson and threatened with a piece of broken plastic rail. These reports paint a very disturbing picture, but, unfortunately, Mr Swanson is, of course, no longer with us, so we can't ask him to justify his actions. The headmaster is still alive, however, and we can certainly ask him to justify the actions he took when he was informed after Peter made his first disclosure.

'There is no doubt in my mind that Peter was telling the truth then, and is telling the truth now. But we need not take my word alone on this. The police interviewed Peter at length before they traced, arrested and subsequently interviewed Henry Sealy. They believed Peter at the outset, and they continued to believe him despite the categorical denial made by Mr Sealy when they questioned him about Peter's statement – a statement taken during nearly five hours of detailed police interview conducted by trained child protection officers. The Crown Prosecution also believed Peter. When they wrote to him explaining why they could not prosecute without further corroborating evidence, they did not say 'the allegations you made', they said 'the offences committed against you'.

'Peter has also undergone detailed clinical, psychiatric and psychological assessment over the past 12 months by qualified clinicians and therapists, all of whom came to the same, unequivocal conclusion – that Peter had been sexually and psychologically abused as a child and the impact on him and his development was, and has continued to be, profoundly damaging. The fact that he learnt to cope with the early effects of the abuse and get on with his life as best he could is a testimony to his courage and to the strength of his character, and it is this that brings me to my second point.

'In 1963, Peter was welcomed into the school as a child of 11, with all of the promise, wonder and potential that lay before him as his mind developed under the staff's care and tuition. He came having worked hard at his primary school where he was assessed under the LEA's five-point scale of assessment as being in the 25 per cent who were above average ability. He also came having shown himself to be a warm and thoughtful child, mindful of others and interested in the world about him. His primary school headmaster, Edward Hunter, who went on to become a highly respected figure in the educational system, said of him at the time: "It has been a continuous pleasure to have had Peter in the school. We wish him well in his future school life and career."

'And so it was that Peter indeed began to show promise and develop further. For the first three years with you his school reports provide the evidence that he was a good pupil. His conduct in that period was described as "excellent" and his headmaster wrote in the second year, "Peter is making very good progress." How, then, was it that this child – for let us not forget that 'child' is what he still was – became a victim – for that is what he became – of a predatory abuser – for that is what happened – while he was under your protection? How was it, then, that when, under the most frightening conditions imaginable, this child came to you for help, you failed him? You failed him, not just in your responsibility for his education, but in your responsibility for his physical, emotional and spiritual well-being.

'For any school to have acted in this way is quite simply totally unacceptable. It is so now, and it was so then. The fact that the school has a Christian ethos makes it not only totally unacceptable, but absolutely unforgivable. Yet, despite this, Peter has told me that he has forgiven you for your failure. What he cannot do, however, is forget, which is understandable. You cannot change the past, but you can change the future. What you should do now is acknowledge what happened, accept that you failed, apologise and learn the lessons. Only then can Peter move on. Thank you.'

A deafening silence filled the room. It seemed to last for a long time. The mediator looked towards me and asked if I wanted to add anything? I took a deep breath and began.

'This has been a very long journey for me, but it is a journey I have to complete. I owe it to Simon, whose death released me from the nightmare, and I owe it to all of the other victims of abuse whose lives, like mine, will have been blighted by Henry Sealy, but who are still too terrified to speak out about the suffering they have undergone because of this cowardly man.'

I paused for a moment, trying hard to fight the emotion surging within me. I really did try, but I couldn't stop it. The hidden pain was finally out and it totally overwhelmed me. The tears rolled down my face and I began to sob. The child inside me that I had protected for all these years was now in front of them once more. The looks on their faces told me they knew that. I continued to speak, the tears still streaming down my face, but my mind became clearer and I felt an inner calm begin to descend upon me. Gradually, that calm grew stronger and I stopped crying, but not speaking. I took them through every aspect of what it's like to be abused and why they must learn from what happened so they don't repeat their mistakes when the next child comes to them and discloses that they are being abused. I finished by saying that just because they have signed up to the latest 'child protection' policies, that does not mean all those who abuse children had gone away.

After a further pause, the older man began to speak in a decidedly shaky voice.

'I was appointed headmaster of your school just after you left. I knew nothing of what you have told us. We can only rely on your word for what you say happened. What I will say is that you should not consider yourself guilty of any wrongdoing. Clearly, something seems to have happened, otherwise you would not be here under these circumstances. We are sympathetic to your pain and we will try to do what we can in light of that.'

The two teachers and the lawyer then took it in turn to talk about how things have changed since I was at school, and how they now have in place measures that would ensure that what I had claimed had happened to me could not happen again to any other boy, at least not in their school. When they had finished, they looked tired and drawn, but their attitude remained defiant and aloof. I felt shattered and very emotional. Judgement Day was taking its toll on me but it was not affecting them in the same way. The meeting was then adjourned for lunch.

After lunch, we reconvened and the subject of compensation was brought up. The mood in the room changed immediately. The limited amount of compassion they had shown previously evaporated completely. Allan asked for a private meeting with their lawyer, and the two men went off into another room. When they returned, having been unable to reach an agreement, the mood in the room became even more depressed, so we broke up and went back to our separate rooms. After about 20 minutes, the mediator came to see us. She looked nervous. She began to go back over the day's proceedings and talk about the importance of me being able to draw a line under the events of the past and move on. She clearly had no idea about the real impact of sexual abuse on children.

Allan, now showing signs of irritation with the woman, interrupted her and asked if they were going to make an offer or not. She paused for a moment and then said: 'Twenty thousand pounds – that's all they can offer.' Her words hung in the air like blue smoke.

'That's ridiculous,' Allan said. 'Their legal fees will be more than that.' He turned to me and said, 'What do you think?'

'It does not sound like an apology,' I said. 'If they really meant what they said today they would have offered a figure that reflected it. This amount is a token payment, not an apology. Go back and tell them that I don't accept their miserable offer and they should be ashamed.' I got up and left the room, followed a few moments later by Michael and Allan. Once outside, Allan asked me if I was OK. I said I was angry and needed time to think. We said goodbye and Michael drove me home. I felt humiliated, but not crushed. My mind was spinning and I desperately wanted to go to sleep; it was the only way I was going to shut out all of the emotions whirling round in my head like a tornado. I told Anne and the children what had happened. They found it hard to understand, but told me not to worry. Something was bound to happen. I went to bed and slept the sleep of the dead.

For the next two days, I sat in my study listening to music and staring out of the window. On the third day, I began to focus on what had happened. I went through in my head the fundamentals of why I had gone back to challenge them. Gradually, it dawned on me that I had been distracted by the money issue. The money wasn't what it was all about. The amount was irrelevant – what I had wanted was something from them that proved I had gone back, faced them down and forced them to put their hands in their miserable, grubby little pockets, hand over some cash and say sorry.

The more I thought about it, the more I knew in my heart that I was right; holding out for a better offer was not on my agenda and never had been. I rang the school's solicitor and explained my position. We talked for about half an hour, at the end of which we had agreed that I would accept their offer and that would be an end of it. I had done what I'd set out to do and even though they had not said sorry, they had recognised that I had suffered, although they had maintained throughout that they had no knowledge of what had happened.

Two days later, he telephoned me and read out a draft agreement to me. It was pretty much as I had thought it would be, with one exception; they wanted me to consider withdrawing the complaint I had made to the police. I was almost speechless – after all they had said in that room about how sorry they were! The spots on the leopard had clearly not changed as much as they had assured me they had.

After a short pause to gather my composure, I told him that by making such a request he was in serious danger of undoing all that had been achieved between us. I felt a growing sense of anger inside but, as I now had all the power, there was nothing to be gained from ranting on at him further, so I explained in the calmest voice I could that to withdraw my complaint would be to turn my back on all the other victims I believed were still out there, too frightened to come forward and disclose their awful secrets.

'Under no circumstances would I betray them.'

He got the message loud and clear, mumbled an apology of sorts and said that it was his job to ask me, but I should not read into his question that that was what the school authorities had wanted.

'In that case,' I said, 'I will forget you ever asked.' He gave a detectable sigh of relief and then he said he would write to me shortly to finalise the agreement.

About a week later, a letter arrived from the school's solicitors. It said simply:

'I now enclose our cheque for £20,000 in accordance with the settlement agreement. This now brings matters to a conclusion and I am closing my file.' The settlement agreement was that I would not sue them or mention them or Sealy by name in any publication in the future.

This part of my struggle was over but, the 'matter' was far from closed. They silenced the child, but they cannot silence the man. It was, after all, Mr Swanson who told me during our conversation that it was my conscience that had led me to the right path.

'Always follow your conscience,' he had told me, 'and in God's eyes you will not be found wanting.' Amen to that, my brothers, Amen! The man with the lamp had returned. The vulnerable little boy inside me that I had protected for all these years could now rest in peace, but the man that child had become still had work to do. I must find the other victims and release them too. This is my destiny and I will not let them down.

13

Moving on

As the days that followed blended themselves together, I felt more and more that I had still not brought closure to everything that had happened. I was still receiving treatment and counselling. I was still broke, having used all of the £20,000 from the school to pay off some of my debts. I had no work and no real prospects that I could see in the near term. But I had learned so much about myself in the process I had been through, and I had received so much love and support from Anne, the children and so many others during my struggle. Surely there must be a way of making something worthwhile come out of it?

The more I thought about it, the more I began to realise that my salvation lay not in walking away from the past, but in embracing it so that others could benefit. I asked myself what I had really achieved from my struggle. Did I get the justice I wanted so desperately? Did I bring my abuser to book? And why did I blame him so much when other men had abused me as well? Why hadn't I challenged them too? Have I really made the journey from victim to survivor, or am I still walking along the road, kicking boulders as I go, angry and frustrated, blaming everyone else for the problems I had suffered? What exactly have I learned from my experiences, and what should I do next?

The answer to these and many other such questions was in truth that I did not really know. The only way I was going to sort it all out was to write it all down. I would let the story tell the story. Only then would I be able to say, 'Ah, yes. Now I understand.'

It took me many more months to find the strength to sit down and begin to write this book as, although I knew I had to do it, the thought of going through it all again was hard to face. But, once I had begun, I could not stop. I knew as I wrote that one day, other victims who needed to release themselves from the pain they carried, but did not know where to start, would be able to read my story and find the strength within themselves to begin the journey out of the darkness and into the light.

There were many more questions I would have to answer before I could finish the story, though. Had I really forgiven those who trespassed against me, or was I just saying that? It has taken me a long time to sort that out, but, in the end, I have concluded that Sealy, and the other men who abused me, will still have to answer for their actions. It is not my responsibility to judge them, nor should I have to. But I can, and should, forgive them. If I can't find it in my heart to forgive them, can I honestly say that I am a survivor? No, I would still be a victim. The way I have come to terms with this dilemma is by accepting that, although Sealy and others caused me great harm, they also, unwittingly, gave me a first-hand understanding of how abusers work, the damage they do to their young victims, and how that damage manifests itself as their victims grow into adults. Having used this understanding in my own recovery, I know that I can also use it to help others recover. So, I am able to forgive them because they gave me such a comprehensive set of unique and powerful tools that I could not have got any other way, which brings me on to the question of my faith. What did all this do to my Christian faith?

The answer is that it destroyed my trust in people in authority. When I took part in Simon's funeral service, I had gone to church for the last time. I hated them, absolutely and completely.

But the years of indoctrination had made their mark on me. It was not quite so easy to turn my back on the Church in the way I had wanted to. I continued to suffer from the awful fear of punishment the teachers at school had instilled in me as a child, and for years I felt unwanted, alone and valueless. My soul was dead. I felt no real emotion within me, I just pretended to the outside world that I was normal, happy and full of life.

As the years went by, though, I became less scornful and over time I developed my own bond with God. I had never been far from God and I found it easy to pray to the God I believed in, who was a God who loved those who could not defend themselves, not a God who sent you to hell for all eternity if you died in a state of mortal sin. I still wanted to be close to God, so I created my own religion, not based on churches or dogmas, or on any of the rest of the nonsense that was how I saw the human-made religions of the world. I created a religion based simply on asking God to help others who were in trouble. It went like this: if I saw someone who had broken down on the motorway, or fallen over in the street, or who looked in need of someone to help them, or even love them, I would say a simple prayer: 'Dear God, please help them.' Five words – my religion was based on just five words, and it worked. It kept me close to God and helped me feel some sense of value and purpose, however small.

When Anne came into my life, I was, at first, scornful of her religion too. She had been brought up in the Methodist Church. In fact, her father was a Methodist minister, a man I grew to love and respect greatly. Her mother was quite simply a saint, and when she died, a great hole opened in our lives. She had been so wonderful to me and our three children when they were young that her loss was a terrible blow to us all. But I have often felt her guiding hand since she died and I know that she sits close to God. I hope and pray that I will one day see her again so I can thank her for everything she did for me.

Anne's faith is strong, but it is not a faith in the Church as an institution. She believes that being a Christian is about how you live your life, not just a way of obedience to a set of rules. She is an inspiration to me and those around her. Anne is a primary school teacher. She teaches children in a very deprived area in north-west England. I see her practise her faith in the way she teaches those young people. She is so patient and caring with them.

Anne has never tried to change the way I feel about religion, but her influence is hard to ignore and I am now able to go into any church with her and say a prayer or sing a hymn. We often visit the cathedral in Liverpool, which is close to where we live, and I have recently taken Communion there.

In saying all this, it would be wrong of me to leave you with the view that I hate the Church, or that I think all Christians are bad. Far from it. The vast majority of church members are good people, and there are many in the Church who do much good work, especially among the poor and the downtrodden. It is more the case that I am still fearful because of what happened. In fact, I am still being treated for that fear using Cognitive Behavioural Therapy. In time, I am confident that I will conquer this fear, but not yet.

In the meantime, I am doing what I believe God wants me to do; helping other victims of abuse learn to cope and make the long, lonely journey to recovery. In 2003, I set up a registered charity called

The Lantern Project with the help of Anne, Michael and two other friends. With the support of a small lottery grant, we created a new web site (www.survivorslantern.org), on which we created a comprehensive library of information covering all aspects of child abuse, its consequences and how to cope with its impact. It also contains the contact details of all the counselling and support groups around the UK and overseas, together with daily news briefings on child abuse arrests, legal issues related to child protection and so on.

Within 12 months, the site had received just under half a million accesses. It continues to receive around 2,000 visits per day, with visitors spending up to 90 minutes per visit browsing its content. It has proved to be of real help to victims, survivors and others who need help and support. When I read the e-mails that some of these people send me having looked at the site, I feel very humble, yet so thankful to have found a way to turn my pain into something so powerful and with such potential to help others who, like me once, had no voice and could not find the way out of the darkness.

Epilogue

So, having told you my story, all that remains is for me to explain the dream about the heron and the kingfisher, although I'm sure you will have already figured it out.

The brightly coloured kingfisher represents the beauty of childhood innocence. We all lose it at some stage in our development, but for so many children it is stolen from us prematurely. The powerful heron represents a child's potential. We are all different so we all have different potential, but, if your childhood innocence is destroyed through abuse, you and your potential are damaged for ever.

The young boy, is of course, me: an innocent child, trusting and full of wonder. The poacher needs no explanation, save to say that evil comes in many forms but there are few that match the destructive power of child abuse. The man in the white robe is also me, but now older, making my journey through life as best I can. The robe is white because it is my shield, it hides the old me, the dirty me, the damaged me, the victim.

The lamp is knowledge – what I learned along the way, which is why I have written this book. I want the knowledge of what happened to me to be there as a record, not to ask for pity, but to help other victims of abuse, both male and female, find the courage and support they will need to recover from their ordeals and survive.

The dream I had as a boy was a premonition of the future. I did not understand it at the time, but I do now. It was showing me that, despite all of the pain, there is still always love, the most powerful and wonderful of all God's gifts, but to feel it in your heart, you first need to find someone to help you understand it. Only then does the darkness go away as the light and the warmth floods in. Thank you, Anne. You are God's love for me.

Useful Addresses

The story told in this book may have affected you personally. It may have triggered memories of experiences you may have had yourself or given you cause for concern about someone else. The following organisations offer confidential advice and support to survivors of sexual abuse and their relatives and friends.

The Lantern Project
http://www.survivorslantern.org

Barnardo's
Tanners Lane, Barkingside, Ilford, Essex IG6 1QG
http://www.barnardos.org.uk

ChildLine
ChildLine - free phone 0800-1111
ChildLine is the free national 24-hour telephone help line for any child in trouble or danger. It is a confidential counselling service offering information and help to children and young people. Lines are busy but keep trying and you will get through.

NSPCC
NSPCC (National Society for the Protection of Cruelty to Children)
NSPCC Children Protection Helpline 0808 800 5000
This is a free national 24-hour service that provides counselling, information and advice.

Stop it Now! UK & Ireland
PO Box 9841, Birmingham B48 7WB
Telephone/Fax: 01527 598 184
Helpline 0808 1000 900